ABOUT THE AUTHORS

The daughter of Harrison Forman,
BRENDA-LU FORMAN was born in Holly-
wood and grew up in Port Washington,
New York. From the age of six, she studied
music and piano intensively for some years,
but eventually gave up her concert ambitions because, as she says, "I'm not single-
mindedly dedicated—and you have to be."
At Barnard College she studied history and
graduated with honors in 1956. Miss Forman's earlier books include a series, "The
Famous First Name Series," for small children. She lives in Manhattan.

A former foreign correspondent for the
New York Times and the National Broadcasting Company, HARRISON FORMAN
has visited almost every country on earth.
Among his early adventures was a stint
as war correspondent during the Sino-
Japanese hostilities in Shanghai in 1932.
Subsequently he managed to be on hand,
with motion-picture cameras, to record the
bombardment of Shanghai in 1937, the
bombardment of Warsaw in 1939, China's
part of World War II, the Japanese invasion
of Indo-China in 1940; the anti-Communist
wars in Malaya and Indo-China and the
Dutch withdrawal from Indonesia in 1950.
More recently, he has traveled throughout
Europe, the Middle East, South America
and, of course, Africa.

Among Mr. Forman's earlier books are
Through Forbidden Tibet, *Horizon Hunter*,
and *Changing China*. His articles have
appeared in *Reader's Digest*, *Holiday*,
Harper's, *Life*, and many other magazines.
Well known as a lecturer, the author has
also appeared frequently on radio and television, on such programs as Town Meeting
of the Air and American Forum.

the
land
and
people
of *Nigeria*

the

land

and

people

of *Nigeria*

by Brenda-Lu Forman and Harrison Forman

Portraits of the Nations Series

J. B. Lippincott Company

Philadelphia · New York

Photographs on pages 13, 14, 19 (a, b, c), 22, 40, 41, 42, 52, 80, 93, 94, 95, 107, 109, 114, 117, 118, 120, 129, 130, 131, 142, 147, and 149 by Harrison Forman.

contents

Portraits of the Nations Series

SAHARA DESERT

- Sokoto
- Katsina
- Kano

NORTHERN REGION

- Zaria
- Kaduna

JOS PLATEAU

Niger River

- Bida

Benue River

WESTERN REGION

- Ibadan

LAGOS

- Benin

- Onitsha
- Enugu

EASTERN REGION

- Sapele

- Aba
- Port Harcourt

L. Chad

REPUBLIC OF CAMEROON

Gulf of Guinea

N

NIGERIA

0   100   200   300
Miles

introduction

ONE OF THE most important developments of the twentieth century has been the creation of dozens of new nations the world over. From Israel to Indonesia, and from Ceylon to Senegal, millions of people have achieved independence and self-government for the first time in recorded history.

The League of Nations in the 1920's included about sixty nations. The United Nations, forty years later, now includes more than one hundred. The passionate feelings of nationalism which created these countries are among the most powerful forces in the world today. We can no longer ignore public opinion in large areas of the earth and presume that their colonial government speaks for them. These new nations are intensely proud of their position in world affairs. They want a place in the sun with all the determination of people who have been denied that place for centuries.

Every young nation faces problems. The United States just barely managed to survive as a united country after our War of Independence. For many years after, our economy was dangerously precarious. But the situation facing today's new nations is even more difficult.

They must create and maintain a stable government. That is

far more difficult now than in the eighteenth century, when there was no Cold War to cope with.

Because they are very jealous of their brand-new independence, the newly independent nations balance delicately between East and West. They do not want outright alliance with either. They fear this would amount to exchanging one master for another.

They must create an industrial society, indispensible for economic and political survival in the modern world. Yet for the most part they have had little if any preparation for it. They desperately need financing and trained people to help them. But they do not want too much foreign aid. They fear that would put them under too great an obligation.

Somehow they must absorb the profound social changes which the twentieth century has brought. Unimaginably ancient beliefs must now be altered to cope with the new order. Sometimes these beliefs cannot stand the strain. When they crack, what is there to take their place? One cannot go back, and yet it is terribly painful to go forward.

But there are good things as well. The white man's technology is a very desirable thing. No nation yet, confronted by the material benefits it can confer, has refused to seek a share in it. The price in social upheaval and economic growing pains is heavy. But it is being paid right now the world over. No one complains that the goal is unworthy. They only complain that the way is very hard.

This book will try to give you a picture of Nigeria, one of these new nations—its history, its problems, its strengths, its weaknesses, and its people. Youth is usually a painful time, whether it is the youth of an individual or a nation. But then it is also a vigorous and exciting time too. Painful or not, no one would ever give it up.

1
getting acquainted

First of all, where is it?

Nigeria borders on the southern coast of the "hump" of Africa, just above the Equator. To the east is the Republic of Cameroon. To the west is Dahomey. To the north are the vast expanses of the Sahara Desert.

The country is named after the great river Niger. With its tributary, the Benue, this mighty waterway forms a huge Y through the heart of the nation. The ancients had heard of it. They called it "the Nile of the Negroes." But until the fifteenth century no white man had ever seen it.

The name "Nigeria" was coined in 1897 in an article in the London *Times*. Until then the different areas had separate names like "Crown Colony of Lagos," "Oil Rivers Protectorate," "Territories of the British Royal Niger Company." The name is almost as new as the nation.

Secondly, what is it?

Nigeria is the most populous single country in Africa. It has about 35 million people. That is about one-fifth the population of the United States. It is a big country too, with an area of 356,669 square miles, which is about one-eighth the size of the United States. From the middle of the nineteenth century

11

until it received its independence in October, 1960, it was a British colony and protectorate.

Thirdly, what is it like?

The answer depends on what part of Nigeria you are talking about. Nigeria is about as varied a nation as you will find. Within its borders it includes a wide variety of climates, languages, and traditions. You must always remember this if you want to understand the Nigeria of today. Only now is this big country learning to feel that it is one country. Nigeria has only a few things which would naturally pull it together and many things which tend to divide it.

Take climate as a start. The coastal areas are hot, tropical, muggy, and heavily forested. The thick mangrove swamps to the east blanket the coast in a tangled, choking mass. It might rain for many days on end here and no one would be surprised. A little farther inland, heavy forests of oil palms cover the country. Endless palm trees produce the kernels which are Nigeria's most important crop.

In the western regions, where it is a little drier, you will see cocoa trees by the many thousands. And here, as elsewhere in this young country, there are still great areas inhabited by few if any people. This is the "bush" country.

As you move farther inland from the coast the land begins to climb. The central portion of the country is a huge plateau with savanna-like vegetation—wide grasslands and patches of forests. This is where the great tin-mine pits are found. The further north you go, the drier it gets. A hot, dry, dusty wind blows from November to April. This is the harmattan. Days here are hot, but the nights can be quite chilly. Trees get rarer and rarer. Buildings are usually made of mud in the north because of the scarcity of wood. By the time you reach the northernmost border, you are right on the edge of the Sahara Desert.

So climate does not help hold Nigeria together. So much variety in the same country means people live in totally different sorts of houses, wear different clothes, eat different foods. It is inevitable that they will have very different points of view.

The United States is much bigger than Nigeria. But if you take a trip across our country, you will feel pretty much at home wherever you go. Nearly everyone you meet in our enormous nation speaks the same language you do, wears the same kind of clothes, and feels he belongs to the same country. It is different in Nigeria. If you were a Nigerian, even a short trip from your home could bring you to a place where you might feel quite foreign among your own countrymen.

First of all, you might not be able to understand them. There is no universal native language. Indeed, more than 250 distinct languages and dialects are spoken. Everybody might speak the same tongue in one area, yet only a few miles away nobody could understand it.

The official language is English, since Great Britain gov-

Modern billboard advertisements emphasize native dress and dialects.

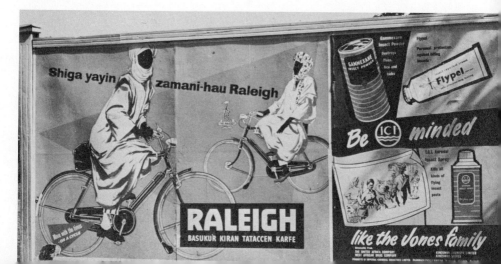

erned Nigeria until it became independent in 1960. English is taught in the schools. You will see it used in newspapers, on road signs, in advertisements and public notices. In the north, however, the common speech is Hausa, the language of the biggest tribe there. Hausa is very popular because it is easy to learn and easily understood. It is written in Arabic characters because the Moslem invaders of the thirteenth century adapted it to the Arabic alphabet.

Inasmuch as there is no common native language to help weld Nigeria together, more and more Nigerians are learning English. If you stay in the cities, even in the north, you can get along very well with English. Outside the cities, however, people still live very much as they did before the British came, and the older people especially often speak only their local dialect. Things are changing, but the change goes slowly.

Arabic is the language of the Moslems in the north.

Pagans, Moslems, Christians—all accord respect to the local
Ju-Ju, *or witch doctor.*

No single religion unites Nigeria. The Moslem religion dominates the north. There are many Moslems throughout the rest
of the country too. Christianity, both Catholic and Protestant,
has many followers in the Western and Eastern regions. And
throughout Nigeria there are thousands of followers of an ancient spirit-worship called animism.

This animism includes many different cults and often varies
sharply from village to village. All cults, however, worship a
pantheon of spirits in nature. The ceremonies strive to put man
in communion with the deities which animate nature, so that the
crops will grow, the children will be healthy, and the tribe will
prosper.

Animism is a very important part of Africa's tradition. To

Christianity is strongest in the Western Region.

the African it is not just a religion to be observed on special days of the week; it is a way of thinking. It is so much a part of him that it cannot be separated from his way of life. That is why an African who has been abroad for study in Europe and America, and who might even be a Christian or Moslem convert, will still often participate in his tribe's animist rituals. It is an act of courtesy to his parents and his ancestors, and it links him to his people's oldest traditions.

Nigerians do not share any common racial origin. America's development in the early days was aided by the fact that most of the colonists came from England or at least from Europe. As isolated as the colonies might have been, they still shared the same overall cultural traditions. That made it much easier to unite as one nation when the time came.

In Nigeria it was just the opposite. Situated astride the middle of the African continent, it has been for centuries a crossroads for population movements. That is why there are so many different languages and customs and habits in Nigeria today. For thousands of years migrations and invasions from all directions have mixed and mingled their peoples and heritages in this area.

There are nine major tribes in Nigeria and dozens of subtribes. Each has its own traditions, and each is proud of its individuality.

You may observe that America has many different national groups, too. But we are still one nation. In Africa, however, ever since ancient times, a man owed his loyalty to his tribe. The tribe's welfare came first.

It had to because survival was so hard. People could live only if they stuck together. But strong traditions like this persist even when they are no longer needed for survival. That is why African nations are still torn by intertribal tensions, even though the causes for them may have been long since forgotten.

Nigeria has not had the terrible intertribal bloodshed that nations like the Congo or Kenya have had. But still the idea of allegiance to a Nigerian nation above and beyond the tribe is a very new one. You who are reading this are probably American. For many generations your people have felt they belonged to an American nation. They considered themselves Americans—not just Ohioans or Californians or Milwaukeeans. A Nigerian, on the other hand, is only now getting used to thinking of himself as a Nigerian instead of a Hausa, an Ibo, a Yoruba, or one of the dozens of other tribes in his country. If you were a young man or woman in Nigeria now, you would be a member of the very first generation which has grown up with this new awareness.

Why did it take so long? The biggest difficulty was communication. Until just a handful of years ago all the various tribes were quite isolated from each other. The thick rain forest in the east made communication nearly impossible. The terrible slave raids, which until the twentieth century were the curse of the whole country, made communication dangerous. When people cannot meet each other, when they cannot speak each other's language and learn each other's ways, they become afraid of each other. They remain suspicious. They herd together in little groups, and it is hard to convince them that outsiders are really just the same sort of people they are.

Since the white man came, communications have improved. Contact with the Europeans widened the Africans' horizons enormously. That is why the southern coastal areas of Nigeria are so much more modern than those in the north. They have had centuries more contact with European traders and the outside world.

But it's been only during the twentieth century that Nigeria has been pulled out of its isolation. Radio, television, books, newspapers, the two world wars, and an all-out educational effort have shattered the tight shell of tribal isolation. And now, also, Nigerians are beginning to realize that their place and importance in the world today depends largely upon their own unity.

By now you can see that there have been few things to help Nigeria unite effectively. You may even be wondering how the country can have any unity at all. It has not been easy, to be sure. But some things have helped.

First of all, there was the English occupation. Without the British takeover there would never have been a Nigerian nation. England took the land and its unrelated tribes and governed them as a unit. Slowly but surely the Britishers welded the country together. If Britain had not created a "Nigeria," Nigerians

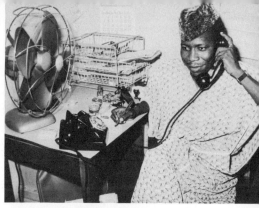

Upper left: *The TV station in Ibadan was the first to be established in Africa.* Upper right: *A Yoruba in native dress conducts business with Western devices.* Lower left: *Modernism—A telephone switchboard operator.* Lower right: *News is broadcast in English as well as in native dialects.*

might never have come to feel they all belonged to the same nation. And there might have been no "nationalist" movement with a demand for Nigerian independence.

The spread of Western customs has helped unity, too. In many ways, to be sure, these new ideas have disturbed African life. They have upset old values and uprooted the Nigerian from his tribe and traditions. They have sometimes set him adrift in a bewildering and confusing world, where he found he no longer knew what to think or believe. But at the same time, the impact of Western civilization has exposed the Nigerian to all sorts of new ideas. It has stretched his horizons. It was confusing at times, but it was also exciting. And it has helped Nigerian unity because Western customs, ideas, and education provided a common ground where Nigerians from widely different backgrounds could communicate with each other. Here was something they had in common which linked them together in spite of the enormous differences of religion, background, and beliefs between them.

In the old days a Nigerian who wanted to be part of the European's world had to tear himself away from everything his parents had stood for. But that is no longer true. In Nigeria and everywhere in Africa today, ancient ancestral customs are being fused with the modern ways of European cultures. Little by little a distinctively "African" way of doing things is emerging— an African style of dress, of literature, of art, and of government, combining both the ancient traditions and the twentieth century.

Nigeria has been very fortunate in its leaders. There have been three particularly important ones. You will find them mentioned in almost everything you read about Nigeria. The first of these is the brilliant and free-wheeling Nnamdi Azikiwe, leader of the NCNC (National Council of Nigerian Citizens) which is the major party of the Eastern Region.*

The powerful, strong-minded Sardauno of Sokoto is leader of the Northern Peoples Congress (NPC). Finally there is the scholarly and dignified Alhaji Sir Abubakar Tafawa Balewa,

---

* Nigeria today is a federal republic of semi-independent states, composed of the Eastern Region, the Western Region, the Northern Region, and the Mid-Western Region, with the Federal government based in Lagos.

Prime Minister of the Federal Republic of Nigeria. These men would be a credit to any nation.

Strong leaders are important to any country. But in young countries like Nigeria they are particularly vital. Countries which have been self-governing for many centuries do not depend quite so heavily on the personality of their leaders. Their governmental machinery is well established and manages to keep going even when the nation's leadership is weak. But young countries just starting out are deeply influenced by the individual personalities of the men who lead them. The new nations of Africa usually have very few people with a Western education and an understanding of their country's part in world politics. So the men who do have this understanding have tremendous influence. That is why nearly every African country you will read about may have only a single central political figure. Often the whole government depends upon him. He holds the country together by his own personality, and if something should happen to him, it may upset the entire government.

In the past few years many African colonies suddenly achieved independence before they were ready for self-government. Nigeria, however, was well prepared for it. The British trained the country for self-government for many years before granting independence in 1960. There are many well-educated Nigerians in the country today. So the nation need not depend so dangerously upon the influence of a single "strong man" or opportunist leader. It is set up so that opposition to the government in power may be expressed within the framework of the government itself. This allows people to feel they have a say in their government rather than feel they are being ruled by one man over whom they have no control. Therefore, there have been no assassinations or revolutions in Nigeria.

Unlike other African countries, Nigeria has no color problem.

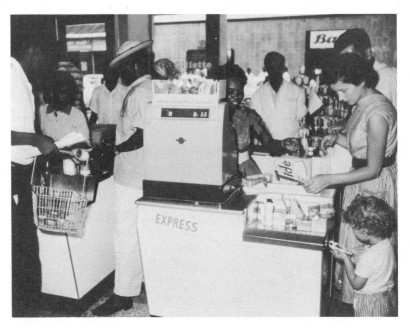

Modern supermarkets are stocked with imported products.

There are few white people. There never were many. To be sure, some Nigerians felt the British did not give them the chance for enough education. They also felt job opportunities for Nigerians were severely limited. Under British rule, however, Nigerians have always had freedom of the press and of assembly.

Color discrimination did exist. But it was not the glaring type found in the Republic of South Africa, where even narrow doorways are sometimes divided into "African" (Negro) and "European" (white) sections. There is, therefore, none of the friction between Negroes and whites as found in South Africa or the Congo. A white man gets no special treatment in Nigeria, nor does he encounter the hostility he so often meets elsewhere in Africa today.

Wherever you travel in Nigeria you will find that the African people are slowly realizing they have an important part in shaping the world's future. This is a very exciting realization. Just imagine what it is like to be a member of a race which for centuries has been conquered, exploited, and cruelly oppressed, considered inferior and incapable of art or culture, even sold like cattle as slaves. Then imagine what it is like to be a newly independent nation with growing importance in world affairs. Think how it feels to be wooed in turn by rival political parties of the very white races who conquered you in the first place. Just twenty years ago few people even dreamed that Africa would or even could be self-governing in this century. Yet in the past decade most of the continent has become independent. The men who lead Africa today are seeing their lifelong dream come true, although they may never have expected to live long enough to see it begin. It is truly exhilarating.

As you learn about Nigeria, therefore, you must remember that this is a young country trying to do two very difficult things at once. It must grow up all of a sudden—build up its industry, government, agriculture, trade, and education all at the same time. And while it is doing this it must play a wise and careful role in the troubled politics of the world today. This dual responsibility means that it must catch up many centuries at home in a few short years, and at the same time it must be a modern twentieth-century nation in world affairs.

It needs patience, courage, assistance—and a lot of money. It needs education and industry. It needs strong leaders and a people willing to work hard to help themselves. Although Nigeria is still a young country, it is already well launched in these areas.

Nigeria is destined to become one of the leaders in Africa's future.

2

its
history

WHY SHOULD YOU KNOW about Nigeria? You may never have heard of it before. Why should you learn about it now?

Nigeria is important because all of Africa is important now. In the last ten years this huge continent has emerged from colonialism. Now it is in the limelight of world politics. Africa is no longer a remote "Dark Continent" on the fringe of our daily life.

Suddenly there are dozens of new nations—Black African nations—in the United Nations. Some of them, like Nigeria, are stable and comparatively prosperous. Others are tiny, terribly poor, and dangerously unstable. But ready or not, they are all independent now, and therefore must be reckoned with in world affairs.

Now African history is very old. But we do not know much about it as yet. We know the continent has been inhabited for as long as—and maybe for longer than—the rest of the world. And we have found traces of great empires which flourished there many centuries ago. But the records of these civilizations have been lost, and so we must reconstruct them slowly and laboriously from archaeological remains.

Nigerian history, on the other hand, is very young. It is the history of an artificially created nation: Nigeria. In less than a century this sprawling chunk of land has been carved out of tropical Africa, and its whole future has been totally remolded into the Western pattern.

While Nigeria was being carved out, little attention was paid to how its peoples were distributed. Nigeria, along with all the other nations of Africa, was visualized as a colony of Europe. Each European power tried to seize as much of Africa as it could. No one thought it mattered in the least how this "scramble for Africa," as it was called, affected the African himself.

Nigeria's boundaries were settled at the conference tables of Europe. As a result, they did some freakish things. On the western side, for instance, they cut right across Yorubaland, leaving a sizable portion of the Yoruba tribe in neighboring Dahomey. Tribal ties, like family ties, are very strong. This then was like splitting up a family. The same thing was done in countless other regions in Africa. Peoples were uprooted from their oldest traditions and set upon totally new and strange paths.

It was the arrival of the white man which started this great upheaval in African history. Gold, ivory, and pepper first brought him to the Nigerian coast. These products brought unbelievable profits to European traders. One thousand per cent was not unusual. But then the profit had to be enormous because the danger was so great. Until the use of quinine to control malaria was discovered in the middle of the nineteenth century, the Nigerian coast was a fever-ridden deathtrap. It was known as the "White Man's Grave."

The Portuguese explored the whole West African coast in the fifteenth century. They were the first Europeans to land in Nigeria. They arrived in 1434 and built up a profitable trade with the state of Benin, which in those days was a powerful kingdom.

The British began visiting the area of present-day Nigeria in 1553, and they soon had the lion's share of the trade. By that time the profits in gold, ivory, and pepper were greater than ever. Then another profitable commodity—the African slave—came to dominate the commerce with Africa.

Columbus made his famous voyages of discovery to the New World in the late fifteenth century. Soon afterward Spain established her great plantations and mines there. These required workers. The local Indians, unused to heavy labor demands coupled with terrible working conditions, died off rapidly, so thousands of Africans were imported to the New World to supply the necessary labor force.

Every year the demand for slaves increased. It reached its peak in the eighteenth century when annually 70,000 to 80,000 Africans were shipped into slavery. Between 1450 and 1850 approximately five to six million West Africans were transported to the New World!

Nearly every European nation engaged in this trade. France did, and so did Spain and Portugal. England and Denmark, who abolished slaving in the nineteenth century, were the most active slavers in earlier times. Our own eighteenth-century Yankee traders also did a brisk business in slaves.

Now, slavery was nothing new to the African continent. It was a very ancient and well-established institution. But the arrival of the European traders made it big business. The African slave dealers had never had such a profitable and inexhaustible market before. They stepped up their activities to a terrifying level.

West Africa became known as the Slave Coast. Entire areas were laid waste by slave raids. Whole towns were destroyed and their inhabitants sold into slavery. In the Middle Belt area of Nigeria you can still see the ruins of towns which never came back to life.

Think what this has meant to Africa. For four centuries thousands of its youngest and most vigorous people were taken away forever. Imagine how this affected African health and heredity. Think of the terrible effect on people's morale. It was often an act of real bravery to venture out of your own village, even if it were no farther than your own fields.

This dreadful trade depressed the whole economy too. Trade and communications could never develop when the briefest journey might cost a man his freedom or his life.

Generations of Africans were robbed of their self-respect as well as their freedom. It left a legacy of fear and distrust which lingers even today.

Toward the end of the eighteenth century, however, an important change took place. Public opinion in Europe began to demand the abolition of slavery. It was wrong to enslave and sell humans like cattle. The Humanitarian Movement, as it was called, grew steadily in influence. Its cause was aided by the fact that Europe, and particularly England, was then in the midst of a tremendous economic change.

This change is now known as the Industrial Revolution. It meant that the old way of life based on agriculture was being replaced by a modern machine technology. The machine was far more efficient than a man—even an unpaid slave. And when machines began to be widely used, slavery in industrialized England and Denmark declined rapidly. The Humanitarians pressed their arguments, and won their way. In 1807 Britain and Denmark forbade anyone to use their ships for transporting slaves.

Britain's political involvement with Nigeria really began here. Until then, Englishmen had restricted themselves to the Nigerian coast trade. But once England was committed to the complete abolition of slavery, she was inevitably drawn deeper into Nigerian political life.

Britain might declare slave trading illegal. But that was by no means the end of the matter. As soon as the British stopped their slave trade in Nigeria, the slavers of other nations rushed in. For in countries which were not so highly industrialized as Britain, the slave trade was still a very profitable business.

England fought for half a century to stamp out slaving along the coast. It was a hard fight, and as she began to win, Britain had to assert control over more and more territory to make sure the slave trade would not be resumed. By mid-century, she was in firm control of the entire coast and the slave trade was dying.

England tried for as long as possible to maintain her influence in Nigeria by indirect methods, since it is very expensive to govern colonies. Annexation was a last resort, and England waited until 1861 to annex Lagos, Nigeria's chief coastal settlement, which had, indeed, been under British control for more than a decade. The important state of Bonny on the eastern end of the Nigerian coast never was formally annexed. But England was in fact the ruling power there from 1835.

Economic reasons soon drew Britain deeper into the interior. After the slave trade had been forbidden, British traders were only permitted to engage in what was then called "legitimate commerce," principally palm oil and palm kernels.

The English were not particularly unhappy about this restriction. Palm produce was a very profitable trade too. The new machines of the Industrial Revolution needed lubricants, and palm oil was important in manufacturing these machine oils. Palm oil was also becoming more and more valuable as an essential ingredient in soap, which until recently had been a luxury. But by the nineteenth century the Industrial Revolution was making everyday life a lot dirtier. Soap, therefore, was coming into wide demand.

Among hundreds of other pursuits, Britain was becoming a giant soap manufacturer. That was why she fought so hard to dominate the palm-product trade in Nigeria.

It was her interest in palm oil and palm kernels which drew her traders deeper into the interior. Previously the British had been satisfied to buy palm produce through the coastal tribal chiefs. But the competition was much greater now, and that drove selling prices down. The English therefore could no longer afford to deal with the coastal chiefs. They literally had to "eliminate the middleman" or else they could not make a profit. As much as these chiefs might object, the English were determined to bypass them and get in contact with the sources of supply in the interior.

Several voyages were attempted to chart the way up the mysterious Niger. But fever killed a terrifying percentage of the men who probed the interior along the great river. It looked as if malaria would defeat the white men entirely.

The turning point came in 1854. The expedition of that year proved that quinine taken daily could both prevent and cure malaria. This great discovery revolutionized trade with the interior. Malaria was not conquered, but it was at least tamed. Trade on the Niger River grew steadily from then on.

3
the
fulani

WHILE BRITISH INFLUENCE was expanding inland from the coast in the first half of the century, a very important thing was happening in the north of Nigeria. The Fulani Empire was enlarging its influence to cover nearly the entire area of what is known now as the Northern Region.

No one is sure where the Fulani come from. Most historians agree they migrated originally from the Mediterranean shores. In the seventh century, soon after Islam was founded, the Arabs swept westward in a tremendous surge of religious fervor. They conquered all of North Africa and most of Spain. The whole Mediterranean world was uprooted, never to be the same again.

The Fulani were one of the countless tribes pushed deeper into the African continent by this relentless Arab pressure. Islam caught up with and converted the Fulani as they drifted slowly southward. They arrived in northern Nigeria about the fifteenth century and settled there peacefully.

As time passed, the original purity of the Moslem government under which they lived in their new home deteriorated greatly. Many of the ancient pagan ways were revived. People started making sacrifices to fetishes again, and women began to discard the veil. This shocked devout Moslems as much as Roman pagan practices scandalized the early Christians. By the end of the eighteenth century thousands of Moslem Fulani were very concerned over what they considered to be the religious laxness of both their people and their rulers.

Their leader was Usman dan Fodio, a Koranic scholar and a man of great piety. His following was such that the Sultan, who lived a luxurious and corrupt life, was afraid Usman dan Fodio might lead his followers in a revolt against the throne.

In 1804 the Sultan of Gobir sent his army against Usman dan Fodio. Even though they vastly outnumbered Usman dan Fodio's forces, they were soundly defeated in the first encounter. Usman dan Fodio then proclaimed a *jihad,* a Moslem holy war, and sent his commanders out to defend the True Faith wherever it was threatened.

Before long they had overrun nearly all of today's Northern Region. Eventually their conquests spread as far south as the border of Yorubaland. They were stopped there by the militant new state of Ibadan. In the east, the Fulani cavalry were rendered helpless in the thick tropical rain forest, so Islam did not penetrate Iboland.

Why was the jihad so successful? The Fulani themselves represented only a small minority of the population. Their military discipline was very poor—on the field they paid little attention to their commanders. They rode to battle arrogantly dressed in their finest feast-day robes, which made it difficult for them to move rapidly.

If they had met any real opposition, the Fulani would never have conquered as they did. They won for two reasons. First, they were the spearhead of a great Moslem reform movement, one similar to that of Christianity's Martin Luther in sixteenth-century Europe. The jihad drew its support from the many Moslems who were angered by the corruption of the tenets of Islam.

Secondly, their Moslem rulers had grown tyrannical and oppressive. The people hated them. The leaders of the jihad, on the other hand, governed honestly and justly, following closely the commandments of the Koran.

But as time passed, the Fulani also grew corrupt and became as bad as their predecessors. When they did, they too lost the people's support. The result was that they themselves were conquered in turn by the British at the opening of the twentieth century.

About the middle of the nineteenth century, Britain and the Fulani Empire were the two big powers in Nigeria. Britain had finally succeeded in crushing the slave trade along the coast. She was in firm control of the whole area included today in Nigeria's Eastern, Mid-Western, and Western regions. The Fulani for their part had consolidated their vast empire and controlled the land that comprises the Northern Region.

The English were very eager for trade with the Fulani rulers, or "emirs" as they were called. The emirs, however, were skeptical about contact with the British. The English were "unbelievers." And as devout Moslems, the emirs would often have nothing to do with them.

Their attitude began to change when they discovered that trade with the English brought them arms and ammunition. Guns and bullets were most valuable, for the Fulani emirs' power depended on military strength.

The British had to handle these northern emirs carefully. In the south when a tribal chief grew rebellious, it was easy for the English to intervene directly and bring him into line. The southern chiefs were not militarily strong enough to resist. It was different with the Fulani. Their states, or emirates, were large and highly organized, each backed by a good-sized army.

The Fulani emirs were proud and easily insulted, and the British had to be careful not to offend them.

With patience and understanding diplomacy, the British managed to open up peaceful trade with the north by the middle of the nineteenth century. The trade soon proved quite gainful because the north was rich. Dozens of new companies rushed to get in on the profits. But there was not enough room for all these new arrivals. Slowly but surely over the next twenty years they drove each other out of business.

By 1879 only one company was left from the shambles. It was headed by a fantastically energetic man named George Goldie. He was a gaunt man with hawklike eyes, irresistible charm, and astonishing powers of persuasion. Until 1900 he and his enterprising Royal Niger Company shaped the history of northern Nigeria.

This company was largely responsible for the growth of British power in the north. It fought stubbornly to keep Germany and France out of Nigeria. It extended British influence steadily deeper and deeper up the Niger and Benue rivers. From 1886 until 1900, it was the government of northern Nigeria, by virtue of its royal charter.

The British Government had been reluctant to grant Goldie's company such a charter, but in 1885, it changed its mind. In that year all the European powers with interest in Africa decided to meet in Berlin to define their "spheres of influence." The "scramble for Africa" was on. Every European power, particularly England, France, and Germany, laid claim to vast areas of Africa.

At the time very little of the African continent was well mapped. These greedy powers then were claiming hundreds of miles of land that perhaps no European had even visited. Nevertheless, they went on drawing borders, arguing fiercely all the way, and giving away unknown rivers and nameless mountains by the handful, with total disregard of the people involved.

At the Berlin Conference Britain claimed exclusive influence on the Niger. Thanks largely to the efforts of George Goldie's company in driving the French off the Niger, this claim was recognized. Britain thereupon undertook to administer the areas in accordance with the agreements reached at Berlin.

But where was the money to come from? The British Government might be ready to declare a protectorate, but it absolutely refused to appropriate any money to govern it. That suited George Goldie very well. He offered to shoulder the cost of Britain's new obligations. His company would serve as the Government's deputy. In return, it was arranged that the company would be given a monopoly on the rich river trade.

The business of boundary-drawing, begun in Berlin, continued right up to the end of the century. The rivalry was intense—and sometimes ridiculous. The English and Germans would get together and settle a stretch of border—and the French would decide they were being ignored. So the French would get together with the Germans and work out a deal excluding the British. That would annoy England and she would put pressure on the French to back out of their understanding with the Germans. And so it went.

It might have been comical if there had not been the danger that this sort of thing might erupt into a European war. It looked that way about 1897 when France and Britain were arguing over their rival claims to the northwestern portion of Nigeria. Although war did not actually break out, it seemed very close for a while.

The Royal Niger Company governed northern Nigeria until

the end of the century. By 1900, however, the job had become much too big for any private company. The British Government, therefore, revoked the company's charter and assumed direct responsibility for the administration of all Nigeria, both north and south.

Frederick Lugard, who later became governor of all Nigeria, was appointed the new High Commissioner of Northern Nigeria. He was a small man with deepset burning eyes, an unbelievable capacity for work, and a will of iron. He had spent years in Africa by that time, and was to spend many more. His contemporaries recognized him as one of the most competent authorities on African colonial affairs. And today he is known as the "architect of modern Nigeria."

No one knew better how to deal with the Fulani emirs than Lugard. He knew when to use force and when to use diplomacy. By 1900 most of the emirs were on more or less friendly terms with the British. But the powerful emirs of Kano, Sokoto, and Katsina in the far north were still dangerously rebellious. In 1902 Lugard decided he either had to subdue these states or see British prestige in Nigeria go to pieces.

Therefore, with his tiny but highly disciplined army, he launched a swift, decisive campaign through the north to bring the troublesome emirates under control.

To the outside observer this undertaking seemed like madness. Imagine! Lugard proposed to pacify this huge area, one-third the size of India, with an "army" totaling 1,050 men and a dozen or so guns. Whereas the three emirates could command some 30,000 horsemen and more thousands of foot soldiers.

The Colonial Office in England was horrified. But it was too late to stop Lugard. He was certain that the Fulani emirs were not anywhere near so powerful as they appeared. He was well aware that the people were indifferent to them, sometimes openly hostile. He also knew their armies were undisciplined and unmanageable.

And he was right. The Fulani armies melted away before him. The towns opened their gates to his men. Kano, Sokoto, and Katsina were taken with scarcely more than skirmishes. With this brief, nearly bloodless campaign, the defiance of the Fulani Empire crumbled. British influence was firmly established throughout all Nigeria. Now began the task of unifying this sprawling land into a modern nation.

4

impact
from
the
west

WE ARE OFTEN PUZZLED—and sometimes annoyed—by the great contrasts between the old and the new in young countries like Nigeria. We become impatient with tradition, inefficiency, or apparent superstition. But we will be more understanding if we stop to think how very many changes these countries have had to cope with in the past half century.

Nigeria became an independent nation in October, 1960. It has a solid economic and political framework, and its future is promising. But only sixty years ago Nigeria was still in the Bronze Age. It had none of the essentials for a modern nation. There were no roads, no industry, no communications. Nigeria was a jumble of completely unrelated societies. Not only did they have no unity, but they had no concept of unity. There was every imaginable physical and psychological problem in the way of making a nation out of these various parts.

Nigeria has had only sixty years to learn what it has taken us over 250 years to absorb. When you think of it this way, you will realize how far these people have come in a very short time.

Do not make the mistake of thinking that Nigeria was primitive before the white man came. It is true there was no industry or machines. But all of the hundreds of tribes had very highly developed social systems. Some of these systems were far more complicated than ours. Tribal traditions set up rules for every occasion. They established correct behavior for any situation a man might meet during his life.

But the white man changed everything. He introduced a whole series of new situations. And tribal traditions often could not cope with these new demands.

From his earliest years the African had been taught to follow strictly these traditions. If he violated any of them, the punishment was severe. But at least he always knew where he stood. Now all of a sudden the wisdom of his tribal ancestors had no answers for him. He was on his own.

This was often very frightening. Sometimes it seemed the whole world was coming apart. What could you trust, when the things you had been taught were most sacred no longer helped you? What could you teach your children when you did not know what to believe yourself?

This was the state of mind confronting the grandfathers of today's Nigerians. Of course the confusion and shock were not always so severe. But to some extent every Nigerian has had to face upheaval in his world. The conflicts still appear. You must always remember that this was a very short time ago. It takes a long time to put two such widely different worlds together so that the seams do not show.

The appearance of the white man was a tremendous shock to the African's ego too. You can understand it more easily if you imagine how we would feel if we were suddenly invaded by a great civilization from outer space; if we, who are so proud of our science and our technology, would suddenly be confronted by a civilization dwarfing ours. Imagine the confusion if our greatest scientists were unable to grasp the fundamentals of the alien technology. And imagine our humiliation if the invaders treated us as children, compelling us, willy-nilly, to change our customs to suit their ideas.

At the beginning of the European invasion the Africans were overawed. As the years passed they became more and more accustomed to the white man's ways, however. They began to learn his skills. Soon many could read and write. More years passed and many Africans were becoming lawyers, doctors, and teachers. The white man no longer seemed such a godlike being. In fact, he had all the human failings Africans had.

The inevitable reaction set in. The educated African was ashamed that his fathers had felt so inferior to the Europeans. He was angry that the Europeans still treated him like a child. Even though he and the other discontented educated Africans represented only a small portion of the population, they soon became quite vocal and very influential. They united to mobilize public opinion behind them and demand a greater voice in government. That was the beginning of the nationalist movement which finally won independence for Nigeria in 1960.

People often talk about how hard it is for American parents and teen-agers to understand each other these days. Nigerian young people often have the same trouble. The world has changed so much so fast in the twentieth century. Young Nigerians are facing a very different world than their parents did when young. Sometimes it is hard to communicate.

Of course, the problem varies from area to area. Deep in the rural areas life has not changed very much. The white man's civilization has hardly touched the isolated interior. Therefore, people go on living as they always have. The young people find that the rules their parents taught them still work. So they do not find it difficult to follow these rules.

But the nearer you get to the cities, the more effect Western civilization has had. Young men and women see the fascinating

Plodding along a trail in the arid Northern Region.

things machines make, and they want to buy them. They see the exciting high-paced life of the cities, and they find their villages dull by comparison. They see the comforts of life that money can buy, but they cannot make the necessary money on their ancestral farms.

The lure of the cities is too strong, so every year thousands of young Nigerians leave their villages or farms and go to the cities to find salaried jobs. But it is not so easy as all that. Nigeria, for all its natural wealth, is still an underdeveloped country. It does not yet have enough industry to absorb all these eager young people. It is very, very hard to find a job. In the meantime, looking for one can be most discouraging.

To add to his insecurity, the young Nigerian may have many doubts about his new life. From the moment he is born an

The pedestrian overpass across a busy street in Lagos.

African is drilled endlessly in his duties to his family and tribe. But when he leaves his rural home for the city, he breaks with this tradition. He is caught in a dilemma. On one hand, he wants to be independent and lead his own life. On the other hand, he feels deeply obligated to send part of his salary home to help his relatives. Naturally there is never enough money to go around. So he is always struggling to make ends meet. This can sometimes be very frustrating.

Life in his family's home is changing too. The very fact that he and so many others like him have left alters his people's daily life. Then when he comes home to visit, he brings all sorts of new ideas back with him. This starts the villagers to thinking. Sometimes it leads them to question the old traditions. Their city cousin might have financial troubles, but he still almost

A modernized "medicine-man" exhorts customers to "Buy Nigerian."

always lives better than they do. It is also a good guess that he exaggerates a bit to make himself look as sophisticated as possible in their eyes.

Sometimes the old ways themselves encourage the change. For instance, throughout tropical Africa when a young man wants to marry, he must pay the girl's family a "bride price." This is a very important custom, for rich and poor alike.

Well, the price of brides has been going up! If a young man wants a wife, he almost has to find a job in the city. He will very likely never make enough money as a farmer. So more boys leave the land to look for a job which will pay them a money wage.

This is the background of Nigeria's development in the twentieth century. You have to keep it in mind as you read on; otherwise, you might think nothing very special was happening. Nigeria's history in this century is certainly not the tale of exploration and adventure it was in the nineteenth century. But under the surface a profound social transformation has been taking place. The things which add up to such fundamental changes do not show much. Social change is the sum of thousands of little experiences in the lives of millions of people. Eventually this means a nation's whole way of life is changed.

5

nationalism

THE MOST IMPORTANT THING to happen to Nigeria in this century was its independence. Since World War I the independence, or nationalist, movement absorbed the energies of all Nigerian leaders.

You might think forty years a long time to take gaining independence. But it will not seem so at all if you consider a few things. For instance, in 1920 the British Government dismissed the very idea of a united Nigeria as a silly dream. Its official position was that Nigerians would eventually become self-governing—but no one could or would say just when this might come about. Everyone just assumed that many years would be needed—perhaps as much as a century.

No one could predict the fantastic speed with which colonial peoples have demanded and obtained their independence since 1950. As late as 1945 even trained and liberal analysts of world colonialism could not see that its end was so near.

For many years the nationalist movement in Nigeria was centered in the cities of the south. Here Western influences had been at work for the longest time. Here Western education was most widespread.

The people in the north were almost totally indifferent to

nationalism. They had had little contact with western ideas. The emirs, indeed, frowned on any nationalist activity. They were suspicious of anything that might disturb the status quo, for it might damage their position.

The nationalists had a double job. It was hard enough to campaign for national independence. Simultaneously they had to educate their countrymen in the very meaning of nationalism itself. They literally had to teach their fellow Nigerians that there was such a thing as a Nigerian nation. Only then could they begin the job of organizing their countrymen to support their demands for self-government.

Why did they bother? We have already mentioned one reason. Educated Nigerians resented their fathers' subservience to the British. They resented being treated as children. Their pride was hurt.

There were other reasons too. Nigeria was administered under what the British called "indirect rule." This system left the traditional tribal governing bodies nearly untouched. They had to report to the British Resident who exercised a kind of veto power. Certain customs such as slavery and cruel religious practices, for example, were forbidden. But beyond that, local authority was left largely intact.

The original idea behind this system had been all right. The British could control Nigeria without disrupting the Nigerians' daily life. It also meant they did not need many men to administer the country. That was good because both men and money were very limited.

It did mean, however, that the "native authority councils" remained rigidly traditional. They made no allowance for the way Nigeria was changing. While more and more Nigerians were becoming highly educated professional people, the tribal chiefs often remained illiterate. The new educated group had no

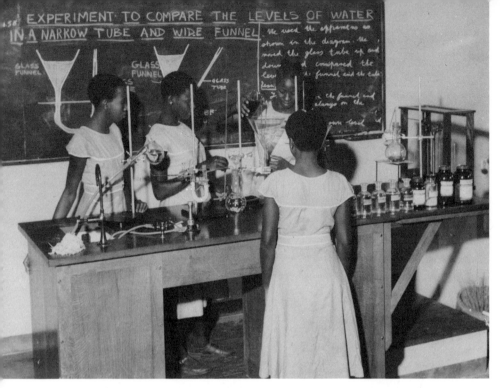

Higher education is now available to women as well as men.

way of taking part in the government through the councils. Naturally they were insulted. They began to feel that the system of indirect rule was only a device to hold the African back by keeping him hopelessly behind the times.

There were still other reasons. A Nigerian working in a European firm received one-third the salary of a white man, even though he performed exactly the same work. In the Civil Service the senior grades were reserved exclusively for white men. Nigerians, therefore, could never rise to positions of authority in either government or business.

Educational opportunities were very limited. There was room for only a relative handful of students in Nigerian universities. Otherwise a Nigerian had to travel all the way to England for a college education. That was expensive. Comparatively few could afford it.

This was a big cause of discontent. Africans craved education probably more than anything else. We Americans take free education for granted. We have been used to it since Colonial days.

To the African, however, education is a golden key. It is the way to a better job, more money, prestige, power, and influence. Until 1956 only a small proportion of the people knew how to read and write. That meant that anyone with even a little education had a tremendous advantage. No wonder young Nigerians would make such sacrifices to get their degrees.

These were the things which made Nigerians resent British control. In the twenty years after World War I the nationalist movement grew by leaps and bounds. By 1937 nationalism was no longer the pet project of a few highly educated "radicals" in Lagos. The government could no longer pass it off by saying it involved a few hundred noisy agitators in a couple of southern cities. Nationalism now included Nigerians from every walk of life.

There were lawyers and doctors and ministers. There were young students returning from their studies overseas, filled with enthusiasm for democratic ideas and contemptuous of the doctrine of white supremacy. There were teachers and clerks thrown out of work by the great economic depression of the 1930's. The groundwork was laid for a new era of nationalism.

In 1937 the necessary leader appeared. The fiery Nnamdi Azikiwe returned to his native Nigeria after eight years of college study in the United States. "Zik" and his followers soon revolutionized nationalism in Nigeria.

Azikiwe was a controversial personality. He was brilliant and capable. He had great personal magnetism. Crowds loved him.

But he was also quite opinionated and stubborn, and he reacted violently to opposition.

Whatever his faults, he quickly became the idol of the Nigerian people. The earlier nationalists had been fairly moderate in their approach. Zik wasted no time on civilities. He launched an all-out campaign against the English. He attacked British colonialism in a chain of newspapers he owned and in his many public speeches.

People found Zik's political approach exciting. He expressed all the pent-up discontent and frustration his people had been feeling for years. He minced no words. His demands were sweeping. He made no concessions to habit and tradition.

His aim was mass public support. No longer was nationalism a movement of the intelligentsia. Zik went straight to the people. He speeded up the pace of nationalism.

World War II accelerated it even more.

It was little wonder that World War II had such a great effect on the nationalist movement. The war shook moral values and ideals throughout the world. It threw Nigeria into much closer contact with the outside world. The result inevitably was that Nigerians were exposed to all sorts of new ideas.

Thousands of Allied troops began to pass through Nigeria when the war spread to North Africa. Nigerian volunteers served in the Allied armies. Both at home and abroad Nigerians were thrown into contact with thousands of white men other than colonial administrators. Suddenly they discovered that the white man was not the godlike being they had been raised to believe. Far from it. He was, in fact, just as human as anyone else. Then what, the African began to wonder, made him superior? Why should he rule over me?

The doctrine of white supremacy was crumbling. The Japanese victories in the Pacific early in the war dealt it a tremendous shock. Colonialists had often justified themselves by saying their rule benefited colonial peoples by protecting them from foreign aggression. But suddenly it was uncomfortably clear that they could not do any such thing. The British had failed miserably to protect Malaya. The French had lost Indo-China. The Dutch could not hold Indonesia. How then could they justify their presence there at all?

People all over the world were questioning the justness of colonialism, not only in the colonies like Nigeria but within the colonial powers themselves. World War II was a terrible time in many ways. But it was also a time of great idealism. People looked at the shambles of the world and determined that they must make it over into something better.

American leaders and the American press criticized colonialism in the strongest terms. The British Labour Party openly denounced it. Their slogan was "Socialism and Self-Government." People everywhere began to doubt the old idea that there were "superior" races which were entitled to rule over "inferior" ones.

When the war ended in 1945, Nigeria was given a new constitution in response to this new tempo of nationalism. The constitution, called the Richards Constitution after the governor of the time, was far from satisfying to Nigeria's leaders. They were angry because the new constitution gave them no real power of decision in government. It had also been put into effect with scarcely any consultation of their wishes. They felt it only gave lip service to more liberal ideas without really changing anything.

But it was a start. In the next fifteen years until independence, Nigeria's constitution was changed three more times until a system was developed which satisfied all parts of the country.

There were many problems to be settled. Nigerians themselves were often bitterly divided on certain issues. How much centralization was there to be? What form were governmental institutions to take? Exactly when was full self-government to be reached? How were the native authority councils to be reorganized? Where would the trained Nigerians come from to take over the British administrators' jobs?

It was difficult problems like these which occupied relations between Nigeria and Great Britain until 1960. But throughout this period the two nations remained on remarkably good terms. The British were wise enough to yield gradually and gracefully to nationalist demands. As a result, the good will between the two countries was preserved. When Nigeria gained full independence, it chose to remain a member of the British Commonwealth.

One thing at least made it easier for Nigeria and Britain to work out such a peaceable solution. Nigeria has no appreciable white settler community. That is, there is no sizable group of white people who consider Nigeria their home. Europeans were never permitted to own land in Nigeria. Nigerians, therefore, never felt they were being dispossessed by whites.

Also, tropical Africa never attracted permanent European settlers. Its soil is not very fertile and its climate is not very healthy. So Nigeria has been spared the bloody clashes which have taken place in Kenya or the Congo, or Algeria, or South Africa. Nigerians feel they own their own country.

In something like a half century, therefore, Nigeria was transformed from a quiet British colony into a strong independent nation. Looking back, you might even say this had been inevitable from the moment of the first white invasion. Once people anywhere realize that a better life exists elsewhere in the world, they will want that life for themselves. They will do whatever they think is necessary to get it. In the end their determination is bound to win out.

6

government

THE UNITED STATES is exactly that—fifty states united under a central government in Washington, (Federal) District of Columbia. Certain matters, such as education, are considered "states' rights." But the final authority in nearly everything else belongs to the Federal Government in Washington. It was this principle of unity under a single central government which was fought over and settled during our Civil War.

Nigeria's government, however, is different. Nigeria is a federal republic of four self-governing areas—the Northern Region, the Western Region, the Mid-Western Region, and the Eastern Region. Each of these has its own legislature modeled on the British Parliament. The head of state is the President of the Federal Republic, but he is more a figurehead than a true executive officer. The most powerful office is that of Prime Minister.

Each region has its own busy capital. Ibadan is the capital of the Western Region, Kaduna of the Northern, Benin of the Mid-Western, and Enugu of the Eastern Region. Each region is entirely independent in all matters of local concern. The decision of its legislature is final on such questions. It cannot be appealed to a higher authority.

The Federal Government in Lagos regulates everything of

national or international concern, such as foreign trade, national defense, and foreign policy. Lagos is the Washington, D.C., of Nigeria. It consists of two islands separated from the mainland by a lagoon. Like our District of Columbia, it forms an independent territory by itself. It does not belong to any of the four regions.

Some governmental matters do not fall easily into either the local or national category. These items appear on a "concurrent list." In case of a question, the Federal Government's decision is final.

This arrangement did not come about all at once. Nigeria

Lagos—Capital city of Nigeria.

had four successive constitutions between 1945 and 1960 before a system was found which satisfied the whole country. The present setup is, in fact, quite decentralized. It has to be so. The earlier constitutions did not work out because they defined a government which was too centralized to fit Nigeria's needs.

Nigeria is composed of dozens of minority groups. There are hundreds of tribes and subtribes. There are scores of local cultures—each with its individual customs and outlooks. They have little if any relation to each other. They probably would never have become members of the same nation if the British had not put them all together.

This big country, therefore, amounts to a collection of many little countries. They fall into major categories corresponding more or less to the four regions. But there are strong minorities within each region, too. The boundaries of the four regions allow for the general shape of Nigeria's diversity. But they cannot provide for it all or else the country would disintegrate completely.

Local governmental traditions are as divergent as possible. The Fulani jihad organized the north into a series of large, strong, semi-independent states, something like Europe in the Middle Ages. Each had its own tax systems, standing armies, and highly organized administrative staffs. Theoretically these emirates owed both political and religious allegiance to the Sultan of Sokoto. But in reality each was almost entirely autonomous.

The Eastern Region's background is just the opposite. The thick tropical rain forest always hampered communications. It made it impossible for the Ibos to evolve large centralized states like those of the open, spacious north. Their government, therefore, developed on the basis of the individual village. Each one was governed by the elders of the community. Each was so isolated in the thick forest that it had hardly any contact with villages only a few miles away.

The Yoruba, who are the biggest group in the Western Region, were not restricted by the heavy palm forests which cover the east. The country is much more open and people could get around much more freely. The Yoruba developed several independent kingdoms, rather like constitutional monarchies. Some of these states became rich and very powerful. But they fought so much among themselves that most of them were ruined by the middle of the nineteenth century. The Mid-Western Region, newly created in 1963, centers around the ancient city-state of Benin, which was rich and powerful as far back as the fifteenth century.

Within each of these large sectional groups there are endless individual variations. There are, moreover, many other tribes besides the ones we have mentioned. Each tribe, even the smallest one, has its own traditions. Each is very proud of its individuality

The English system of government has been superimposed on all this variety. Many Europeans were doubtful during the nationalist period that the institutions of British government would be at all well suited to Nigeria's needs. But in the end they were proved to be the best available solution. If the constitution had tried to provide for all the local variations in government traditions, the result would have been chaos.

These very old native traditions do not always combine easily with the newer British system. All sorts of conflicts arise.

In government, for instance, what is to be done with the tribal chiefs? They do not really fit in anywhere. So Houses of Chiefs are provided for in the constitution. But they are only a partial solution. It is a waste of good leadership to ignore them. The people are still very loyal to them. But what is the best way to integrate them into the modern government?

Law is even more complicated. Here Nigeria really lives in two different worlds. The English extended British Common Law over all Nigeria as it came under their control. But ancient customary law was preserved in cases concerning marriage, the family, land tenure, inheritance, and chieftancy disputes. British Common Law was applied in these cases only where customary law was found to be "repugnant to natural justice, equity and good conscience."

This can become very complicated. Customary law is unbelievably varied. It differs sometimes from village to village. It is hardly ever written down, so it can be a task in itself to discover exactly what the traditional procedure should be. The court must then decide if this procedure is "repugnant to natural justice." "Natural justice" is a rather vague term, so this leaves room for a lot of variation in interpreting the law.

Take marriage, for instance. You may get married according to the Marriage Ordinance, which follows British law. Or you may marry according to customary law. Customary law often allows a man more than one wife. But both forms of marriage are completely legal just as long as you do not mix them. Islam permits the Moslem in the north to have as many as four wives if he likes. That is the limit set by the Koran. In other areas a man traditionally may have as many wives as he can afford. And all his wives are equally legal wives. He will not be guilty of bigamy unless he also marries a woman under the Marriage Ordinance.

That might seem reasonably simple. But it does not stay that way. Suppose, for example, that a man marries his wife under the Marriage Ordinance and then dies, leaving several children.

Who inherits his estate? His wife? By British law, yes. But if his relatives choose to contest the estate, customary law might provide them grounds.

Perhaps the man had married another wife by customary law and had children by her. Customary law recognizes these children's claim to his estate. In some areas a man's brother inherits even before his children do. If an inheritance is contested, the court must decide which type of law to invoke. That is not always an easy decision.

A distinctively Nigerian law is in the process of formation right now. It is evolving gradually as British Common Law and African customary law blend more and more. Every time a difficult case is decided, it creates a precedent which will make it easier to decide the next one. It just takes time.

7
the
regions

THE OUTWARD FORMS of government are fairly uniform throughout Nigeria. The legislatures are set up similarly. The government bureaus and officers are organized along the same lines. But the real *practice* of government varies a great deal.

As with everything in Nigeria, the difference is particularly marked between north and south. The north is much more authoritarian than the three southern regions. It is governed more by its traditional ruling aristocracy than by the people. The emirs are firmly in power as they have always been. The ideas of democracy are still too new to have had much effect.

Many things uphold the conservatism of the north. One is the Moslem religion. Islam is a fatalistic belief. People tend to accept the way things are because "it is the will of Allah." They do not get upset easily about oppression and injustice. Only if they feel their religion is in danger do they become violently angry. Otherwise social reform or political causes do not gain wide support.

Islam also emphasizes close observance of authority. Moslem society is strictly stratified. It is very hard to move up from the class you are born into. Young progressive thinkers have difficulty finding popular support for their ideas. Unless they are

Pomp and ceremony attend the movements of a Moslem dignitary in the Northern Region.

aristocrats, people consider them upstarts. There is much pressure from both people and rulers to maintain the status quo.

There have always been many Moslem schools. But Moslem education teaches only religion and the study of the Koran. It does not teach English. It ignores the modern world completely. Moslem students, therefore, come out of school with almost no awareness of today's world. They have not been trained in the vital basics of reading and writing. They have not been exposed to the revolutionary ideas which are changing the world so rapidly.

As Western education spreads, however, so do Western ideas. Moreover, the north has begun to realize that it must become more modern in its outlook. Otherwise it will rapidly fall behind the south, which is much more advanced in both politics and education. The rivalry between the Northern Region and the other regions provides a strong incentive for modernization.

The whole atmosphere in the Western, Mid-Western, and Eastern regions (collectively considered Nigeria's south) is different. It feels much freer. It is more democratic in our sense. There are two important reasons. First, Yoruba, Edo and Ibo traditions are very different from those of the north. Secondly, they have been exposed to European influences far longer than the north.

We have described northern society as being very strictly stratified. Ibo, Edo and Yoruba societies are not nearly so rigid. Ibo tribes in the east were governed by councils of the eldest and most prominent members of the village. Any man could work his way up to a position of authority if he wanted to. In that sense, the government was very democratic. A man might become a great warrior or a rich farmer or a powerful medicine man. If he was determined, he could reach the top in his tribe, even if his father was poor and obscure. It was easy to adapt this system later to one modeled on English local self-government.

It was not quite this easy to work your way up in the Yoruba and Edo kingdoms to the west. But even here all power was not concentrated in the chief of state as it was in the north. The king was certainly powerful, but so were the leading noble families and the religious priesthoods.

In addition to the difference in traditions, there was steady contact between the southern areas and European influences for over four centuries before the north was even touched. Nineteenth-century British trade with the north, on the other hand, was strictly confined to the banks of the Niger and Benue rivers. The Fulani emirs would tolerate no interference in their government. They would not permit foreign missionaries to tamper with the True Faith of their subjects. While Britain controlled the south quite firmly long before the nineteenth century was over, her influence in the north, even as late as 1902, was almost nonexistent except in the region of the river banks. One rebellious emir encouraged his people to defy the British by declaring that an Englishman was a species of fish and would die as soon as he was taken away from the water!

Even after the British pacification of the north in 1902, there was very little to upset its rigid organization. The British made a point of interfering as little as possible in the government. The north was to be the showcase of "indirect rule." British supporters were installed as emirs. They had to govern according to the advice of the British Resident. But he was careful to intrude as little as possible.

This system functioned efficiently and inexpensively. But the restriction of the north's contact with the outside prevented it from growing into the modern world. At the height of the nationalist movement in the 1950's the north woke up to find itself far behind the south in political development. Self-government was at the door and the north suddenly realized it was seriously unprepared for it.

A terrific dispute developed between the north and the south.

Britain had agreed to grant self-government in 1956 to any region wanting it. The two southern regions wanted self-government immediately. The north, however, was reluctant. It realized it did not have the trained administrators necessary for self-government. The north feared, therefore, that as soon as the British left, it would be completely dominated by southerners.

The debate about self-government raged hotly in the newspapers and at the constitutional conventions. The southern papers ranted at the northern leaders. They called them "imperialist stooges," "slaves of foreign domination," and such things. The northerners were naturally deeply offended. Their fears of the south increased. It became all the harder to reach agreement on the issue.

There were serious riots in Kano in 1956 and many people were injured. It looked for a while as if the north might secede altogether. Eventually a compromise was reached. The north finally set a date to request self-government, and the southern regions postponed their request a year. Complete independence came in October, 1960. We hear so much these days about nations which demand immediate self-government that it seems odd to hear of a nation which nearly divided because part of it did not want self-government.

Disagreements like these sometimes threaten to tear the new African countries apart. There are thousands of tribes on the continent. There is often much rivalry and distrust among them. Nigeria's own unity emerged only from a difficult period of hot dispute. Some nations, such as the Congo, have had to shed much blood before unity could be achieved. Others are only precariously unified. Yet in spite of such discouragements, many African leaders dream of unifying the continent into a great United States of Africa.

It will take enormous determination and effort. Nonetheless, the dream may yet come true. The African nations have much to gain from unification. Nigeria has a rich potential. But many others are tiny, economically unstable, and shockingly poor. Individually they have very little influence in world politics, united they could be both strong and influential.

Like all such things, it will take time. Unity takes practice. Nigeria's own unity started shakily. But each year it is strengthened as the country gets used to working together. Each year, too, more Nigerians have come to realize how much their international prestige depends on their remaining a united nation. If enough Africans begin to see the advantages of joining and working together, the future may very well see a United States of Africa.

8

precious
education

NIGERIANS, LIKE MOST AFRICANS, want education more than almost anything else. Ever since the white man came, education has symbolized the road to prestige and success. From the beginning the British Government needed Nigerian clerks. But they had to be able to read and write. It was the same with the European trading firms. Thus a Nigerian who was educated became a man of importance among his people. He was in close contact with the all-powerful British. He was a man of influence. And it was education which made him so. Naturally, everyone wanted this valuable learning too.

It was the church mission schools which first spread Western education throughout the southern areas of Nigeria. Until 1956, indeed, they were about the only Western-style schools in Nigeria. Because missionaries were strictly excluded from the Moslem north by the terms of the treaties with the emirs, it fell far behind the south.

The Christian mission was always both church and school. Christianity and education went hand in hand in Africa. But a lot has changed in education since those early days. Now schools stress the things which will enable a young Nigerian to earn his living. They give him the vital basics of reading and writing, and try to teach him a skill which is needed in his country.

In the early days the missionaries' idea of "civilizing" the African was to make him as much like a white man as possible. They taught him the English language and literature and European history. Africa was considered to have no history of its own. African culture was presumed to be nonexistent. The African himself was taught little which had any immediate application to his own life. He was bombarded with bias and attitudes about the inferiority of his whole heritage.

To be "civilized" he had to dress, speak, and act like a white man. They demanded that he renounce everything associated with his tribal life. He must not use African given names. He had to give up dancing and native music, which were considered "pagan" and "immoral."

This meant he had to cut himself off completely from his own people. A hundred years ago, this did not seem a bad thing. The people of the nineteenth century had an overwhelming faith in Western "progress." They considered material advancement to be the proof of a superior civilization.

And since the Africans did not have highly developed machines and industry, their civilization must be inferior. So it seemed correct to measure an African's "cultural advancement" by his success in turning himself into a white man.

But what resulted was an imitation white man, not an educated black man. The African tried to ape every aspect of European life. And of course he made blunders, because these things were unfamiliar to him. The white man would smile condescendingly at the African's clumsiness and use it to justify his opinion that the African was childish and inferior. A reaction was inevitable and natural. We have already seen that it played an important part in the independence movement.

Education in Nigeria has changed much during our century. But it is still a magic key to an immeasurably fuller life. Without an education, jobs are difficult to find. With an education, everyone needs you. A young Nigerian will make enormous sacrifices to gain a university degree, or even a high-school diploma. In the south, parents spare no pains to send their children to school. Sometimes a whole village will chip in to send its most promising student to college abroad. He is considered a community investment. A good education will make him valuable, and he will repay his fellow villagers when he returns and becomes a successful man. Even in the north today, Western-style education is beginning to spread because the young people there want it so much.

No one studies so hard as a young African when he goes overseas. He will stay for years sometimes, accumulating degree upon degree. Among educated Africans it is nothing unusual for a man to hold several Ph.D.'s—in law, engineering, economics, agriculture. A student will work at anything to keep himself at school. The famous Nnamdi Azikiwe himself worked his way through Lincoln University in our south as a janitor and dishwasher.

The mission schools did much to bring education to Nigeria, but they could not possibly handle more than a small percentage of the country's population. In 1956, therefore, the Nigerian Government began a crash program of universal primary education. The aim was to teach every Nigerian, young and old, how to read and write.

Six-year elementary schools were established throughout the country with government aid. As you might expect, most of these were in the south where a Western education was in the greatest

A primary school class receives instruction under a tree in the Western Region.

demand. In 1962 the first group of "school-leavers," 200,000 strong, obtained their "Standard VI" certificates and went out to seek their fortunes in the world.

This has had far-reaching economic repercussions. Before the days of universal education most of these young people would have remained on their ancestral farms. But now they feel that is not good enough. They are now "educated." The cities fascinate them. And the lure of a salaried job adds excitement to city life. Many feel they would do almost anything rather than return to their villages and become farmers again.

At present Nigeria does not have enough industry to absorb all these eager young people. Some three million dollars has to be invested in Nigeria to provide jobs for only three hundred people. There is not that much money available. So there are not nearly enough jobs to go around.

This is not fully appreciated as yet. Only a short time ago a Standard VI certificate was rare enough to guarantee a job to anyone who had one. Most people still think this is so, and they are often baffled when they find it difficult to get a job in the cities, even with a school certificate. One firm, for instance, advertised a few positions open. In one week 4,000 people applied. A town in the Eastern Region advertised for a few girls as trainee nurses. A thousand applied in three days.

A mother attends an adult education class in the Western Region.

Why doesn't the "educated man" want to be a farmer? To begin with, a farmer in Nigeria has very little prestige. Under colonial rule no important man worked with his hands. Colonial officials never performed manual labor. For the young African, then, the desk, a white shirt, and a necktie are the outward symbols of success.

Nor is farming in Nigeria today a way to make money. The average farmer still uses ancient tools and antiquated methods. Naturally his living is poor because his techniques are so inefficient. What is the use, a man will ask, of getting an education unless he can become a success? Everyone expects him to justify his education—his parents and his village may have made great sacrifices to pay his way through school. To the African, becoming a success means making money—and that eliminates farming.

Actually they are not really against being farmers, but against being farmers in the old-fashioned way. If farming could be made more profitable, many of these young Nigerians would be more than eager to take it up.

This requires two things: training in modern farming methods and an opportunity to use them.

There are a few government-operated agricultural training schools, but not enough. Every year thousands of young Nigerians apply for entrance. But only a few hundred can be enrolled. This training program must be expanded. But that takes money. The government simply cannot find the money for everything all at once.

Meanwhile the relatively few boys who graduate from these schools have only limited opportunity to put their new knowledge into operation. They cannot change the whole agricultural system unassisted. They must re-educate their fellow farmers. It takes a while to make the average Nigerian farmer aware that better methods even exist. Then he must be persuaded to use them, for he will not change his ways until he is convinced he can make a better living by doing so.

There is also the problem of money. Modern farming requires modern equipment, and that is expensive. Where do you get the money? The government will loan it to the training-school graduate, and he can pay it off over a period of ten years. But this is a very expensive program. Thousands of Nigerians might want to take advantage of it. But there is only enough money for a few.

An eager young farmer in Nigeria also meets other problems. For instance, who actually owns the land? Since time immemorial, except in the Moslem north, land has been owned collectively by the tribe. A farmer might have the use of it, and he might pass his "right" on to his descendants. But no one person could ever say he alone owned the land.

The educated young farmer, however, will want to be able to say he owns his own farm. Otherwise what incentive is there to mortgage his future to buy the expensive equipment he must have? The type of land title we know is only now coming into use. Even now it is used only in certain parts of the country. In the end, therefore, the whole system of tribal land ownership must be reassessed. And like all such great changes, that takes time.

In the meantime some very modest agricultural programs have been quite successful. In the Eastern Region, for example, the government has started a chicken-raising program. Hundreds of Rhode Island Red hens have been imported. This is a sturdy, disease-resistant breed which is much better than the native variety.

A government worker will teach a group of women how to care for these properly. If the women observe certain conditions, they may keep the chickens without cost. One important condition is that each woman must teach ten other women what she has learned.

This sort of program which requires no education is what Nigeria needs most today. It is designed for illiterate country women who are eager to improve themselves but cannot afford elaborate and expensive programs. The small slow gains these programs achieve eventually add up to big changes.

Nigeria is fortunate not to be dependent upon a single crop. In addition to its three major crops—palm kernels, peanuts, and cocoa—Nigeria exports rubber, cotton, bananas, soybeans, and citrus fruits. The hides and skins from the north bring high prices overseas. Valuable tin comes from the central plateau around Jos. Columbite, a mineral once thrown out as waste in tin mining, is now an essential for making stainless steel and heat-resistant alloys for jet engines.

This sort of diversity is bound to bolster Nigeria's economy and help bring stability to its government. All its eggs, so to speak, are not in one basket. A one-crop country like Cuba is beset by severe economic difficulties if its one crop (sugar) does not sell profitably. When the economy is in trouble, the government is too. When people are hungry, unemployed, angry, and confused, dictators and "strong men" move in.

In addition, it is vital to Nigeria's future that it develop its own industries. Nigeria needs industry to give its people jobs and to manufacture the machinery and goods necessary to improve their standard of living. Farmers need home-manufactured machinery which they can afford instead of the expensive imported equipment they cannot buy.

Nigeria has a good start. There are plants for extracting palm oil throughout the country. There are peanut processing plants in the north. There is a large citrus fruit cannery in tropical Ibadan, and a candy factory in Kano, almost on the edge of the Sahara. There is a big plywood and veneer factory at Sapele, a large textile factory in Kaduna, breweries at Lagos and Aba, a cement plant in the east and a corned-beef cannery in the north. Cigarettes are made at Ibadan and Zaria, using Nigerian tobacco. And retreading worn-out tires imported from abroad is a big local industry.

So you see Nigeria's industry is definitely launched. But look carefully at the list above. There is no heavy industry. There are no steel mills and no factories making heavy machinery. Oil was recently discovered in the Eastern Region and a big refinery is now being completed. The coal fields around Enugu are well developed. But this is only the beginning. All of Nigeria's rich resources are still waiting for proper development.

An agricultural country like Nigeria must inevitably develop its heavy industry. If it does not, it will have to import all its basic machinery. That is very expensive. Right now Nigeria depends mostly on the United Kingdom or West Germany for its machines. It must import almost all its manufactured goods, machinery, chemicals, and motor vehicles.

This is not a very favorable situation. The raw materials Nigeria exports sell for low prices. The industrial goods it imports demand high prices. That is why Nigeria knows it must develop its own industry if it is to survive.

But heavy industry takes money—a lot of money. So the old question repeats itself: Where is it to come from? There are not many Nigerians with the sizable capital needed. Those who do have it prefer to put it into trade where the profits are quicker.

The answer, then, is foreign capital. Nigeria does everything it can to interest foreign investors. The United Kingdom has

always helped with extensive loans, and Nigeria could not have developed as far as it has without this aid. But it takes a lot more money than that.

The government has given encouragement to foreign capital by offering tax exemptions and other inducements. Good profit-sharing terms are proffered to those who undertake to develop the country's natural resources, all of which are government owned. Each region retains a public relations counsel in the United States, and his biggest job is to attract American capital investment.

Capital is not the only thing in short supply. Modern business and industry must have trained managers and technicians. There are still not enough Nigerians fitted to fill these positions. So a great many of them are filled by Europeans, particularly British.

Left: *A skilled worker on a machine in the Odutola Tyre-Retreading Factory in Ibadan.* Right: *The study of electricity is featured in the College of Arts, Science and Technology, in Zaria.*

Nigeria needs all the educated technicians it can get. It needs trained people with basic skills who can teach their skills to as many others as possible. It needs plumbers, printers, metal-workers, carpenters, and agriculturalists. It needs engineers, teachers, and economists.

Training like this is invaluable in a new undeveloped country like Nigeria, and young Nigerians go everywhere in the world to get it. They attend universities in the United States and England. They enroll in the German Institute for Developing Nations in West Berlin. You find studious young Nigerians in many countries of the world. But they always return home. Because nowhere in the world will a young educated Nigerian have such a future as in his own country. He is in terrific demand. One young American, a typographer, recently moved permanently to Nigeria. His reason? "In America," he said, "I was just another member of the union. In Nigeria, I can run my own company and do the kind of work I really think is worth while."

So it is money and education which Nigeria wants most of all now: money to build its industry and education to train its people. It has a very promising future. Its government is stable, its economy is well grounded, and its people are eager to help themselves.

9
the
people

COAST TO COAST, and from Maine to Florida, Americans wear just about the same kind of clothes. But Nigerians have dozens of traditional dress styles. You could never tell a New Yorker from a Chicagoan by looking at his suit. But you can tell a Yoruba from a Fulani right off.

Many African and Asian peoples have given up their native dress and adopted Western fashions. And particularly in the cities, one sees many Nigerians wearing trousers and shirts, or Western dresses. But most Nigerians prefer their own colorful native costumes. Especially since independence, they are taking pride in these handsome, brightly colored clothes.

Traditional dress is perfectly acceptable everywhere. People wear it to work, to parties, or out shopping. Even at formal diplomatic receptions it is as correct as a tuxedo or an evening gown. It is fascinating to see a woman in a splendid evening dress dancing with a Nigerian in his brilliant flowing robes.

Nigerians love bright colors, so a Nigerian street scene is much more colorful than any you would see here. Yoruba girls from the Western Region usually wear a loose-fitting, scoop-necked blouse, with a sarong-like skirt of printed material wrapped around the waist and tied in place. A stole is draped gracefully around the shoulders and a "head-tie" completes the costume.

Even little girls wear the "head-tie." This is a length of material tied around the head in an elaborate fancy pattern. Every girl invents her own style. Sometimes it is simply wrapped around her head. Usually it is wound so that jaunty ends of the fabric stand up like feathers or wings.

Nigerian girls in the south love jewelry, too. They wear a lot of it—in beads, earrings, and all sorts of shiny ornaments. The Yorubas of the Western Region are particularly fond of the color blue. A great deal of the cloth they use is made in varying shades of it. In the north, red and yellow are the favorites, although the blue cloth of Kano is very famous.

Children enjoying a comedy in an outdoor movie theater.

A Yoruba, wearing the traditional decorated cap and robes.

Yoruba men from the Western Region and Ibo men from the Eastern Region wear loose-fitting trousers with long billowing robes in diversified styles. Fabrics with brightly printed or woven designs are preferred. Sleeves are cut loose and full to cover most of the arm, but they can be caught up at the shoulder, leaving the arm free. When they are worn this way, the material falls in extremely graceful folds. A small neat pillbox-shaped hat, tilted forward at a jaunty angle, completes the costume. Sometimes for certain occasions the whole outfit is in white, which looks particularly handsome against the Nigerian's dark skin.

Many Nigerians—both men and women—go barefoot. They can even play football barefoot! After all, it is never cold in tropical Nigeria, so a lot of the time one does not need shoes. Many people wear sandals with soles cut from pieces of an old automobile tire. This makes a very springy, comfortable shoe, which will almost never wear out.

The north is something of a contrast. Northern Nigeria is different from the two southern regions in many important ways. One of the first things you would notice is the way people dress. The north is nearly solidly Moslem, and has been so for some seven or eight centuries. Moslem men dress often in white. They too wear loose, flowing robes. But these robes give more the impression of long loose coats than the tunic-like style preferred by men in the south. Many wear large turbans with a tail of fabric which they draw across to veil the lower part of their face. An important official like an emir will dress in heavy magnificent robes for state occasions. The Moslem religion,

Most high officials in the Northern Region have been educated in England.

however, frowns on luxury and display. So many times a man of means will deliberately dress austerely.

The Koran, the sacred book of Islam, enjoins every pious Moslem to make a pilgrimage to the Holy City of Mecca at least once during his lifetime. This used to be a difficult and dangerous journey northward across the great stretch of the African continent to the Arabian peninsula. It could take years to complete. A Moslem who did so gained great dignity when he returned. Nowadays it is an entirely different matter. Great airliners fly planeloads of pilgrims to Mecca and back within a few days. But the pilgrimage is still an important obligation to every Moslem. After he returns from Mecca, he will wear a white skullcap to show he has fulfilled this command of the Koran.

Northern women live very differently from those of the southern regions. If her husband is rich enough to support her, a married Moslem woman almost never goes out in public. When she does, she will wear voluminous dark veils which completely conceal her from head to toe. Only her eyes are left free so that she can see where she is going. The poorer Moslem women must go out and earn money selling snacks and other things in the streets. But you are not likely to see a well-to-do woman in your travels in the north, unless you are invited to someone's home. Even then, the chances are you will not see them unless you yourself are a girl. The only men who may visit a married Moslem woman are her relatives or her husband's relatives. All other men are strictly forbidden to see her face or even talk to her.

The Hausa and Fulani tribesfolk of the north are very devout Moslems, although the Fulani tend to be more pious than the Hausa. They are also the ruling class, in spite of the fact that the Hausa outnumber them. Nearly all the people of northern

Nigeria are either Fulani or Hausa. They still consider themselves different from each other, but actually they live very similarly. They even look much alike because they have intermarried so much in the past 150 years.

But one branch of the Fulani lives an independent wandering existence. They are the "Cow Fulani." And while most of them are Moslem, they differ in nearly every other way from the rest of their tribe. They are nomadic herdsmen, always moving from place to place with their cattle. The girls do not wear veils. They braid their hair in long plaits with colored orna-

The famed longhorn cattle in the Northern Region.

ments woven into their hair. Often they wear beaded boleros and leave their midriff bare. The men braid their hair, too. Usually they wear a simple robe fastened over one shoulder and go bare to the waist.

The Cow Fulani's whole life is centered around his cattle. He loves them deeply and treats them more like children than livestock. Their cheese and milk is much prized in the north. The Cow Fulani do sell meat from their herds, but they never eat it themselves.

Their skill with cattle is legendary. They are said, for instance, to know of a secret cattle trail extending uninterrupted from the far north right down to the coast. When the tax assessor approaches, it is said, they will call out to their cows, and the whole herd will thunder down and sweep off with them. The Fulani will be right in the middle of the stampede, talking to their animals and actually directing them, while the tax assessor stands helpless in the dust.

The Cow Fulani look very different from their fellow tribesmen. That is because when the Fulani first came to northern Nigeria, the Cow Fulani kept themselves apart from the people they found living there. The "Town Fulani," on the other hand, settled in the inhabited regions and adopted many of the Hausa customs. They intermarried freely with the Hausa, and that is why the Hausa and the Town Fulani have much the same physical characteristics. The Cow Fulani, however, never marry outside their tribe. They have preserved the original distinctive Fulani features. They are tall and slender, with straight black hair, fine reddish-brown skin, and well-modeled features. They almost look like ancient Egyptian paintings.

Westerners tend to think of Africans as looking very much alike. But nothing could be farther from the truth. Nigerians, like Americans, come in all shapes and sizes, and quite a few colors too. The coastal peoples are usually very dark-skinned and somewhat stocky. The pagan tribes of the Middle Belt are often small and wiry. The Fulani of the north are slim and tall, with reddish light skins. In between there is every possible variation. You will see tall Nigerians and short ones, thin ones and fat ones, black, bronze, copper, brown, and tan ones. They have long faces and wide ones, beaked noses and broad ones.

Don't forget that many strains have contributed to Nigeria's heredity, as they have to ours. African peoples crisscrossed Nigeria for centuries. There are thousands of Near Easterners from Arab countries living in the southern cities, where they are often rich traders and merchants. Europeans have been coming and going in Nigeria for some four centuries. Nigeria is as much a "melting pot" in its way as our United States.

You will notice in your travels that a great many Nigerians have patterns scarred on their faces. Sometimes the scars are just simple lines. Sometimes they are elaborate designs covering the whole cheek. You can see these facial scars in the photographs of many African leaders. They are called "tribal marks."

Tribal marks were originally a method of identification. Every baby was given the marks of his clan at birth. As soon as you were born your face was cut in a certain pattern. Each tribe had its individual design. Mud was rubbed into the cuts to keep them from healing, until finally clear scars were left.

These tribal marks were a surefire identification card. You could never lose them. They could not be forged. They were immediately visible. They made it possible for you to tell a fellow tribesman on sight, and he could recognize you too. This was important because the tribe was the center of your loyalty. If you could not immediately tell another of your tribe, you might risk killing him in battle. Or if you were traveling, your

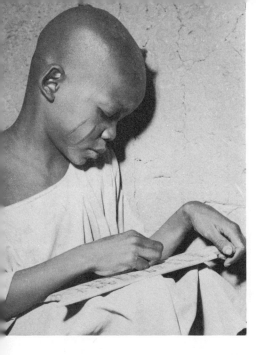

The pattern of facial scars identifies a person's tribal origin.

fellow tribesmen might not accept you and you would starve or be killed.

The tribe has always been deeply important in African life. That is true even now in spite of the spread of western ideas and culture. The tribe was your father and mother and family. It demanded your loyalty throughout your life—but it also cared for you all your life. It was security and comfort and belonging. It was protection against the frightening unknown world outside. Its "medicine" shielded you from the hostile sorcery of rival tribes. Its gods, or *jujus,* supported you as long as you were faithful to them. If something went wrong, you knew you had offended the juju. The tribe's cult prescribed a remedy—although sometimes it was a terrible remedy. The Ibos, for instance, considered the birth of twins a dreadful event. It was a sign that the gods were very angry. Twin babies were literally thrown away.

Tribes do not necessarily live together in the same place, but they do consider themselves descended from the same god. They actually are closely related by blood.

But tribal organization has changed. Today no one in Nigeria can be isolated as he used to be. The tribe can no longer be self-contained. It cannot shut out the rest of the world. Many of its young people go to the cities for jobs or overseas for education. Even those who stay home have radios, read magazines, and see airplanes, movies, and motor trucks. They have become part of the outside world now, no matter where they are or how isolated their dwellings.

So the tribe's organization must and does adapt itself to the changing times. Tribesmen living in the cities have organized clan unions to help out their freshly arrived fellows. Very slowly, Nigerian life is being reorganized. As young Nigerians travel more and become more educated they begin to want more out of life. The old narrowly confined world of the tribe is not wide enough for them. They respect its family loyalties and its ancient traditions. But more and more they are combining these with their new ideas and ambitions.

You can see it in the way they dress. Leaders in the southern regions often wear traditional dress for public occasions—but they wear Western-style shoes with it. Many Nigerians will combine elements of both—the men a traditional tunic with a pair of Western-style trousers, the women an African wrap-around skirt with a Western blouse. Many of the new dress styles for women deliberately combine both Nigerian and Western influences.

10

the
arts

NIGERIA IS SOAKED in music. Every wedding, funeral, or festival is an excuse for exuberant dancing and singing. Drummers wander through the marketplace. A little boy with a tiny drum will collect a crowd in the street. Music and rhythm are part of the Nigerian people's heart.

The drumming gets into your blood. West Africans are the most dazzling drummers in the world. Drums are everywhere in Nigeria. You cannot escape them and you cannot resist them.

Nigerian drums come in all sizes. There are great signaling drums, six to eight feet long, made of hollowed-out tree trunks. There are cylindrical drums covered with stretched skin at both ends. There are drums you sit on or clasp between your knees. There are drums you sling over your shoulder, and tiny hand drums which make a pattering sound. There are deep bass drums and bell-like tenor drums. There are drums you play with your hands, and some you beat with sticks, and the royal kettle drums of the north which are struck with thick lengths of tough rope to announce the approach of the emir.

The Yorubas of Western Nigeria have drums called "talking drums," made of two cone-shaped frames joined together tip to tip. The bases of the cones are covered with stretched skin.

Cords are run loosely from end to end, forming the sides. The whole thing is suspended from the player's left shoulder and struck with a curved stick he holds in his right hand. By pressing with his left elbow on the drum's side, and altering the pressure of his left hand on its head, he can change its pitch.

These drums can produce so many different tones that they sound amazingly like the Yoruba language. Indeed, it is not too difficult to understand and interpret what the drums are saying if you try hard enough.

African music was the ancestor of our own American jazz. When your feet start twitching and you can't sit still listening to an especially good piece of jazz, you will know what it is like to hear African music. The rhythms are very, very complex, with interweaving syncopations and complicated cross-patterns. But the effect is utterly direct. It gets inside you. The drums and singing seem to pick you up and sweep you away.

The most amazing thing about it is that Nigerian musicians do not rehearse. No one writes down the music for the players to learn. In fact, it would be nearly impossible to write down this music. It is too free to fit into rigidly defined bars; instead, the music is almost composed as it goes along. It never comes out the same way twice. It's rather like a jazz jam session. The players all share the same musical traditions. With such a common ground to start with, they doodle around a little and before you know it, they are playing full tilt as though they had been together for years.

You might not appreciate the singing immediately. It is very different from our style of singing. The vocalist uses his voice differently. Sometimes it might sound harsh or shrill to your ear. If you listen carefully for a while, however, you will begin to appreciate it. And sometimes it can be most lyrical and wonderfully sweet. A Yoruba song mourning the tragic death of Dag

Hammarskjöld is hauntingly lovely. There are many others just as beautiful.

Songs are about as fluid as the rest of Nigerian music. Anyone who feels like it makes up a song, and anybody who feels like it adds to it. Songs are always being composed. They grow and incorporate parts of other songs. Parts of them may be taken out and adapted to older songs, or turn up as the basis of brand-new ones. Nigerians sing while they work as well as when they play. So there are songs for every occasion.

There is a special sort of song called a "praise song." It is set to your own individual rhythm and describes how beautiful you are, or how talented, or how brave and famous your ancestors were. The praise singer is an important part of the festivities, particularly in the north of Nigeria. He is usually a fine drummer and the people give him money to sing their special songs. Sometimes they toss coins to him. Sometimes they go up to him and paste the coins on his forehead where they cling in the perspiration. Often the boys will compete for the favor of a pretty girl. Each one will try to give the praise singer more money to sing about how beautiful she is.

And there is always dancing. People dance when they feel like it—when the singing and the music move them. They make up their own steps if they wish. A dancer can become so carried away that he is nearly hypnotized, while the onlookers clap the rhythm and watch absorbedly.

Hear how poetically this verse from a Yoruba wedding chant describes the feeling of this dance: "A lady is just about to dance. Her waist already begins to dance. Yet she herself has not started to dance!"

In addition to spontaneous dancing, there are hundreds of ancient traditional dances for special purposes. There are wedding dances and funeral dances, rain-making dances, courtship and harvest dances. Each one has its own special chant and its individual rhythm for the orchestra.

As with music, no one records the dance steps. No one teaches dancing. Every boy and girl has grown up with his people's music. He does not need to be taught. Music and dance are part of his blood. That is why you will find very few professional performers. Very rarely do dancers and musicians get up on a stage and play for a seated audience. Instead, everybody is really a performer. Everyone grows up that way. The audience is

Yoruba women dancing the "High Life."

part of the performance itself. There is no neat line of footlights separating them.

There is "ballroom" dancing, too. Go to a night club in Lagos on a Saturday night, for example. The very air has a holiday feeling. Nothing blasé here. People are having fun. The band is playing loudly with an infectious shuffling sort of calypso beat. And everyone is doing the High Life.

Supposedly, it takes two to High Life. But when you really get going, you don't have to take this rule too seriously. In fact,

Northern tribesmen in full regalia.

if you get enthused with your own dancing, you could ignore your partner completely. No one would be surprised—so long as you keep dancing. Anyway your partner might be ignoring you.

Like a lot of good dances, the High Life step is basically very simple. All it really amounts to is shuffling in time to the music. But the step is only the beginning of the High Life; the heart is the movement.

And do they move! Bottoms wiggle, shoulders shake, heads nod ecstatically—not frantically because the rhythm is not that fast, but easily, happily, and humorously. The High Life is just about the friendliest dance around!

Eventually the band stops playing High Lifes. Immediately the dance floor empties except for a few European couples dancing a foxtrot or two. Everyone knows this set is just to give the dancers a rest and a chance to order some more beer. A few minutes later everybody is back to High Lifes again.

A Nigerian orchestra includes many instruments besides drums. There is, for example, a huge xylophone made of thick wood blocks. There are dozens of flutes of different sizes. They are usually made of wood, with finger holes cut into the bore.

In the north the Hausa have a wide variety of stringed instruments. This is a result of the strong Arab influence on northern culture. Arab music uses stringed instruments much more than drums. The most popular among the Hausa is the one with only a single string and a very simple fingerboard. But when you hear it played, you would be amazed how versatile it can be.

Then there are the magnificent seven-foot-long trumpets which herald the approach of a great emir. These beautiful instruments are plain, slender shafts of metal with a narrow bell at the end. There are no finger holes. The pitch is changed only by the player's lips. A parade of proud, turbaned trumpeters in their voluminous robes sounding a fanfare for a royal party is one of the most impressive sounds and sights in Nigeria.

Everywhere in Africa storytelling is a very old tradition. Folktales are close to the African's heart. The storyteller is a much respected person. Children will sit around in the evening and listen to him for hours. Adults are just as fond of a good tale. Some stories have choruses in them where all the listeners join in.

Storytellers do not make up their tales. Far from it. The folktales are all very well known to the audience. They have been passed down for centuries and most people have heard them from childhood. A storyteller's art is in breathing life and vigor into an old tale. Sometimes he imitates the different characters. Sometimes he acts out all the scenes. Listeners ask for their favorite stories just as you would ask a vocalist to sing your favorite tune.

African folktales are about magic and wonderful happenings and how the world came to be the way it is. Many of them resemble Aesop's fables. Animals are the leading characters and there is always a moral at the end. There are many stories about enchanted animals which turn into humans—usually beautiful women for the hero to marry. There are innumerable tales of witchcraft and sorcery, as well as ghost stories.

A favorite character in Nigerian folklore is the tortoise. He is wise and wily. He is the animals' leader, but he often outsmarts himself. He is a trickster, but he sometimes gets caught in his own trickery.

Nigerians are artists at music, dance, and stories of imagination. So it is no wonder that they are artists at other things too.

In the old city of Benin, now capital of the Mid-Western Region, you will see some of the finest bronzes and ivory carvings in the world. Back in the fifteenth century, when the Portuguese

*The wood-carvings of Benin
are world famous.*

first came to Nigeria, they found Benin already a rich and powerful state. Its artisans made many exquisite statues and vessels for
their ruler. In later years the city fell upon bad times. The
priesthoods became too powerful. They demanded more and
more terrible sacrifices. They made war on neighboring states
for slaves.

Finally, in the nineteenth century, the British decided Benin
must be subdued. In 1897 an expedition entered the city. There
they found such a scene of bloodshed and human sacrifice that
Benin became known in Europe as the City of Blood.

But the British also found the marvelous works of Benin artists. The design and execution of these bronzes and ivories are so fine that many Europeans of the time refused to believe Africans had made them. Instead they maintained they must have been done by fifteenth-century Portuguese artists working in Benin!

Now, of course, everyone recognizes the richness of African art. It is highly valued all over the world, as you will realize if you try to buy it! You can see many of these art treasures in the museums at Benin and Ibadan. Many are no longer in their native Nigeria. After the 1897 expedition a great many were

Bronze figure of an ancient Oni (ruler) of Ife.

taken to European museums. Sometimes the head of a figurine will be in one country and the body of it in another.

Needless to say, the Nigerian Government makes a great effort to find and conserve its art treasures. Not only are these things beautiful, but they are helpful, too. Africa has very few written records, so historians study these ancient discoveries closely to help reconstruct Nigeria's past.

Rewards are offered to anyone who finds an artifact of the past. You never know where one will come to light. It may turn up when a house is being built or when a road is being laid. Many such treasures have no doubt been destroyed because the workmen did not know what they were.

Wall decorations in Kano include geometric designs, animals, birds, even airplanes.

Recently tin miners on the Jos plateau discovered a rich find of very old terra cotta figures buried in a deposit of black, tin-bearing sand. A whole series of very beautiful heads come from Ife, located in the Mid-Western Region. The Yorubas say the first man came to life there. Its lovely terra cottas and bronzes are as famous as the Benin bronzes and ivories.

Nigeria has many handicrafts too—useful things made by hand and ornamented to make them beautiful. The carved calabashes of Oyo are famous. The calabash is a kind of gourd. When dried and hollowed out, it makes excellent bowls, baskets, and containers. The Oyo carvers ornament them with gay, colorful, complicated geometric designs.

National Hall, off Tafawa Square in the heart of Lagos.

Beautiful handwoven textiles are made in many parts of the country. The patterns are woven into the fabric in some cases and printed on at other times. The deep blue cloth from the dye pits at Kano has been especially well known for many centuries.

There are fine leatherworkers in the north because there are animals to supply the skins. The metalworkers of Bida are famous for their beautifully worked bowls and trays. And there are hundreds of other small individual artisans working all over the country.

Art, you see, is much more a part of everyday life in Nigeria than with us. When we want to hear music, we usually turn on the radio or play a record. A Nigerian is more likely to make up his own song. When we want to dance, we go to a "dance," where we follow the steps someone taught us. Or else we go to the theater where a trained performer does our dancing for us! Nigerians, on the other hand, dance easily and naturally—and just about everyone is so good at it that Nigerians are not much interested in professional performers.

We are so used to mass-produced things that we have nearly forgotten how to make something by hand. Our clothes, dishes, and buildings have all begun to look alike. The tradition of individual workmanship has largely died out here. But in Nigeria you will find hundreds of signs of individuality—in a hand-printed head-tie, in a carved calabash, in a gaily painted mud house, or a splendid camel saddle.

It all makes Nigeria a colorful place to be. The diversity which has caused problems for Nigeria in the past still makes it a fascinating and varied place to visit and study.

11

a woman's world

WHAT IS IT LIKE to be a woman in Nigeria today? What is her status in Nigerian society? How has it changed, and how is it changing with the times?

Like everything in the nation, it depends on what part of Nigeria you are talking about. The north and south differ in many ways, as we have seen. The difference is especially pronounced where women are concerned.

Nigeria has always been a man's world. It still is for the most part. But women in the south have always had a lot more freedom of action than in the north where Islam dominates. The traditional culture of the south is more liberal toward women. And the long-term European influence on the two southern regions has had a big effect on the status of women.

Missionaries, for instance, made a strong point of monogamy. Christian converts were only permitted one wife. Naturally a woman who is the only wife in her household has a lot more prestige than one who must share the house with several others.

Also when British women came to Nigeria with their husbands, their marital example had a strong influence on Nigerians —in the cities, at least. Everything about the British was new and surprising—their clothes, their food, their behavior—and their women were too.

Women in the south are often successful traders. From the time the British arrived, many southern girls were able to go to school. Those who were converted to Christianity took part in their new religion on a basis of equality with their men. Today women in the two southern regions have many freedoms, including the right to vote. In the Northern Region, on the other hand, only men have this right.

In the north, as you know, Islam is supreme. In most Moslem cultures the status of women is traditionally low. They have no legal rights as we define them. Only the wealthiest girls are able to obtain an education. Their marriages are arranged for them, and they may never see their future husbands before their wedding day.

Many girls in the Northern Region are still strictly secluded (in *purdah*) after they are married. And marriage comes when a girl is only fourteen. After she enters her husband's home, she must remain there more or less permanently. She may visit relatives at night, and she may have family and women friends visit her at home. But she is not free to move about in the outside world.

When a northern Hausa girl gets married, the ceremony is marvelously complicated. It can go on for weeks before she is considered properly married. First, there are the preliminary formal visits by the families with exchange of gifts. For many days the bride is ritually washed and her nails and skin stained pink with henna. This is considered very beautiful among the Hausa.

On the actual wedding day everyone gets into the act—all the relatives, all the bride's and groom's special friends. There is no end to merrymaking, joking, and teasing, as well as dancing, singing, and drumming.

Everyone has fun, except the bride. During the whole marriage ritual, down to the day she finally enters her new home, she is expected to weep and wail and pretend great reluctance about getting married. Even if she is willing, she must not appear to be. It is not considered proper.

Once she is married, she spends nearly all of her time in the women's quarters of the house, or "compound" as it is called. But she is not completely dependent on her husband as she might be in other Moslem countries. She makes snacks at home for sale—millet balls, roasted peanuts, bean cakes, and things like that. The little boys and young unmarried girls peddle them for her in the marketplace. She can weave at home too or raise goats, also to be sold at the market.

It usually happens that the richer and more prominent a man is, the more strictly secluded he keeps his wives. It is a sort of status symbol. It was not so easy to keep your wives at home in the past, particularly in the rural areas. They had to go out to draw water or gather firewood or help on the farm. Only a rich townsman could afford to keep his women at home.

Now, however, the women do not need to do these tasks. They can have water and wood brought right to the door. All they require is the money to pay for it. So the women themselves sometimes promote the strict observance of purdah. If people see them working outside their compound, it means they do not have the money to pay to have the work done for them. And they do not want to be thought poor.

There is plenty of company in the compound, however. The husband of the house, all the wives (the Moslem religion allows each man up to four), and all the children, along with some older relatives, live together there. The whole place is called a compound because an entire family lives together in a collection of huts around a common courtyard instead of in one large house. As a matter of fact, most West Africans prefer this arrangement, and group living is typical of all parts of Nigeria.

A Hausa compound is a large space with a wall around it. Inside it is divided by another wall into two main areas. You enter through a gatehouse in the outer wall. This leads into the outer courtyard. The young unmarried sons sleep here. Then there is another gate in the inner wall. That leads into the inner court where the women live. No men except the husband of the house and his kinsmen are allowed in here.

Let us assume we are all girls, so that we may go inside for a closer look. It is not an impressive sight. But it is not meant to be. A collection of neat huts stands around the court. There may be some goats and chickens about, which will eventually be sold at the market. Each wife has her own hut. She sleeps there with all her young children. If all the wives cook together, you might see a kitchen shed. Otherwise, each wife has her own cook fire outside her hut.

The husband spends a night with each wife in turn in her hut. When he is there, the children sleep in one of the other huts. Sometimes he has his own sleeping hut in the women's court. Then each wife comes to him in succession. The wife who is spending the night with him is responsible for cooking his supper.

Now this arrangement does not result in the jealousy you might expect. A Hausa girl does not think it a bad life at all. Her co-wives share the housework with her. That leaves her more spare time to make pin money by weaving, embroidering, cooking, and so forth.

The first wife has seniority, no matter what her age. Old or young, if she arrived first, she takes precedence. All the others follow her in the order they arrived in the house. This eliminates jostling for position. The husband is expected to divide his time equally among his wives. In most cases, provided he himself is fair, the women get along together perfectly well.

Of course if he starts favoring one wife, he is in for trouble. The other wives will gang up on him. Being henpecked by four wives is no joke. But when it does happen, usually he has no one but himself to blame. Islam is decidedly a man's religion. The girls are raised all their lives to obey their menfolk. If a man cannot be master in his own house with this kind of backing, it is a good guess he is either weak or unwise.

What this arrangement does result in is your being related to a lot more people than in our culture. You have some three times as many cousins because your father may have three other wives besides your mother. Then there are dozens of other family ties which are considered extremely important, to which Western cultures pay little attention.

For example: your mother's elder brother and your father's eldest sister are special relations. Everyone has several "fathers" because all your father's brothers are called your "fathers." Not only that, but all your mother's sisters are your "mothers." And all your first cousins are your "sisters" and "brothers." This is just the beginning. And even when he is very young, every child is expected to know and understand all the complicated family relationships he is heir to.

To us it might seem strange to address an aunt and an uncle as "mother" and "father." These relatives rarely seem so close to us. But a Hausa does not merely use the names; he behaves toward these relations as though he really were that closely related. If you were a Hausa, you would not just *pretend* you had several mothers.

There is a whole set of manners each child must learn for use with various relatives. Some, for example, are "joking relations."

Whenever they meet, they are expected to tease each other and play pranks. Children and their grandparents are joking relations. A wife jokes with her husband's younger brother, and a husband with his wife's younger sister.

There are also "avoidance relations" who must avoid each other's presence and never use each other's name. Parents, in public particularly, although to a lesser extent in private as well, must avoid their first-born child all their lives. The mother never touches or fondles her first child in public. The very youngest child, however, is its parents' special playmate.

All this seems very complicated to us, but the Moslem Hausa take endless interest in it. They dearly love to trace the interweaving patterns of kinship. They enjoy intensely the complicated etiquette required on various occasions.

A Moslem Hausa girl's first marriage is usually arranged by her parents. Very seldom is she able to marry the man of her choice. But divorce is suprisingly easy. So a girl might remarry three or four times later in life.

Why does she marry so young? Because as soon as she is ready to bear children, she is expected to marry and begin raising a family. The Hausa consider it quite unthinkable that a mature girl should remain unmarried. Even when she divorces her husband, it will be for another man, not to live a single life. A woman, the Hausa believe, should be having children. That is her role.

The whole custom of polygamy stems from this point of view. Polygamy is an important part of traditional African culture. It is also a very ancient custom in many other other parts of the world. Its original purpose was to make sure no woman remained unmarried and childless for lack of a husband. Children were precious. So many children died in infancy that a tribe could not afford to have the child-bearing years of any woman go to waste. There were usually fewer men than women in the tribe because many were killed in war or on the hunt. So it was quite natural that a multi-wife system should develop.

From the most ancient times, children have been a symbol of success and happiness. You can read it in the Bible and in hundreds of other ancient sources. Millions of people today have no understanding of the world-wide threat of overpopulation. But they do know that for thousands of years their ancestors have measured success by their flocks, their fields, their wives, and particularly their children. It is terribly difficult to convince these people that their numerous children are now more a threat than a blessing.

In Nigeria even a senior wife loses much of her authority if she bears no children. She is treated with respect, of course. But everyone knows she carries less weight with her husband than her co-wives with children of their own.

The Moslem Hausa are a very large group in northern Nigeria. That is why we have described so much of their life. Along with the Fulani, they dominate the Northern Region. But a word of warning must be put forward here. Do not forget that there are many variations—that you can make very few generalizations about Nigeria. The worst thing you can do is to apply what you have learned about one group to all of the others.

For example: There are pagan Hausa as well as Moslem Hausa, although not so many of them. There are many individual pagan tribes in the Middle Belt. There are the Cow Fulani as well as the Town Fulani. The Cow Fulani live a nomadic life, as you have already read, while the Town Fulani live very much like the Hausa.

Then you must remember that this traditional life is slowly changing as western customs spread. The custom of polygamy, for instance, is very slowly but surely dying out. For one thing, it is expensive. Bride prices keep going up, not to mention the cost of supporting a wife once you marry her.

But more important is the growth of westernization. Only in the deep rural areas has the traditional culture remained undisturbed. The closer you get to the cities, the greater are the changes which have taken place. European manners and ways are gaining more and more ground among Nigeria's young people. Even though they retain their religious beliefs, they increasingly adopt Western ways of life.

Educators from India teach in Nigeria's higher institutions.

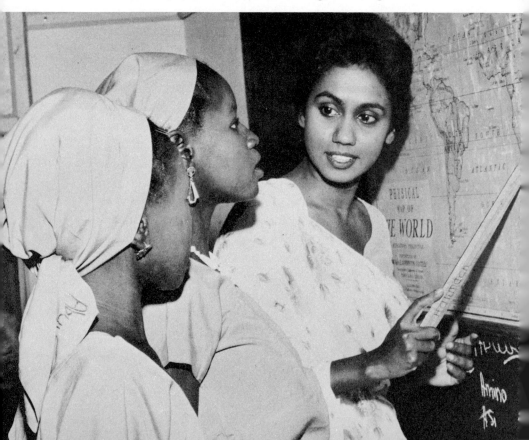

As you can guess by now, this is more true of the south than the north. But even the north is beginning to change. Until a few years ago, for instance, southerners and Europeans in the north had to live outside the city proper in the *sabon gari,* or "strangers' quarter." The *sabon gari* was quite a contrast to the quiet, rather sedate city itself: with all its fantastic mixture of people and backgrounds, it was a lively, harum-scarum, exciting place. But northerners were strongly discouraged from going there by the emirs, who did not like their people to have much contact with outsiders.

Now, however, this is changing markedly. There is more and more contact among the various groups—and thus less and less suspicion. The north has launched a huge educational program, just as the two southern regions have. Little by little its people are learning about the rest of the world.

Here and there women are coming out of purdah. Some are going to school. Changes like these are very hard to get started. But once they begin, they go faster and faster. So in a few years you may find many changes in the girl's life, about which we have talked here. The world changes more rapidly each day, and Nigeria's young women want to be part of it.

12

a
boy
of
the
ibo

YOU ARE A BOY from the Eastern Region. You are an Ibo, which means you are a member of the most numerous tribe in that area. You live in the palm belt in a simple village of mud huts with thatched roofs.

Perhaps one of your richer neighbors has a tin roof on his house if he has traveled a bit in the outside world. But for the most part your neighbors and your clan and all your ancestors have lived in the same village as far back as anyone remembers.

Your parents probably do not know how to read or write. They have rarely been out of the village. But they will make certain that you go to school. They know school is the road to a job and a better life. They are determined that you complete your six years of elementary schooling and get your Standard VI certificate. Only a few years ago this simple certificate was sure to get you a good job in the cities because so few people were educated at all.

There are hundreds of new schools now. Some of them are mission schools. But more and more of them are being set up by the government. The teacher is a very important person in the village, although he might have had only six years of education himself. Teachers are needed so badly that sometimes it is enough if he can teach his students how to read and write.

Your parents are simple folk. They have had practically no contact with Western civilization. There are even some villages where no one has ever seen a white man. The villages are so isolated in the vast lush tropical rain forest that the white man never came there. For centuries your people have raised their yams and kola nuts, and harvested their palm kernels. Even the arrival of the white man did not change their life much. It is not a luxurious life. But it is a simple and enduring one.

Your village believes in *jujus*, the spirits which animate nature. They must be given proper respect. Even a villager who has traveled—who may even possibly call himself a Christian or Moslem—often retains in his heart this ancient belief. When

A native hut in the Northern Region with a meal ready for the family.

he comes home to his village, he makes sure to see the rain-maker and he is careful to pay his respects to the village spirit.

It is wonderful how your people are combining their ancient beliefs with the new modern civilization. In many other parts of the world, the old traditions have gone completely to pieces when modern culture arrived. But Nigerians are combining both worlds with great success. If they like, young people can really have the best of both worlds—the security of their ancestors' traditions and the new benefits of Western civilization.

Your parents pay your school fees. If they cannot afford it, your uncle may do so. If he cannot, another relative or member of the clan will pay them. The system of tribal obligation is very extensive. Sometimes it is hard for Westerners to understand this. It is like a very large family. You are responsible for the whole clan's welfare, not just your immediate family's.

Your father, let us say, might have owed your uncle a favor. You therefore may help your uncle's children in return, because your father's original obligation extends to you. Later, if you get a job in the city, you will send part of your money home. The money is not just for your own relatives; it is for the common benefit of the entire village.

You attend school for six years and obtain your certificate. Then, like thousands of your young countrymen, you leave your village. You want to find a job in one of the big cities.

But jobs are extremely difficult to find. Factories are rare. Business cannot supply enough jobs. You can spend months looking in vain for work.

The situation, however, is certainly not hopeless. True enough, it turns out to be nearly impossible to find a job in industry. But in the back streets of the city there are hundreds of small independent tradesmen—dozens of tiny businesses: tailors, car-

A side street in Lagos.

penters, metalworkers, and craftsmen of all sorts. You become apprenticed to one of these and begin to learn your trade.

But you do not make any money as yet. How do you live then? You live with your "brother." He is not necessarily your blood brother. In fact, usually he is not. He is your clansman. He comes from the same village or group of villages you do, and he will house and feed you during your apprenticeship. Later, when you have established yourself, you will do the same for one of your younger "brothers."

Your clan's organization has expanded greatly to cope with

the changes in Nigerian life. When you leave your village, you do not lose its protection and guidance. Your clan has a "branch" in the city. It is there to meet you when you arrive. It takes you in, introduces you to your fellow clansmen, and helps you get launched in your new life.

Once a week in the city the "clan union" holds a meeting. It is a very businesslike affair. Minutes are taken of the proceedings. There are clan officers—a president, secretary, and so on. All clan affairs are regulated at these meetings. If one of the members has misbehaved himself, he is reprimanded—perhaps even fined. Money is collected for members in financial need. When you are ready to take a paying job, for example, the clan union and your "brother" will finance you.

You will, you see, be expected to pay a fee to the person in charge of hiring. If it is your first job, you may not have the money to pay this fee. The clan union will pay it for you. It is a loan, however, not a gift. You must pay it back in installments out of your wages.

Being an Ibo, you are very likely to become a merchant. Ibos are known as the nation's traders. They have a long tradition of hard training in commerce. They had to become good businessmen, for the soil of the Eastern Region is too poor to grow enough food for its people. Ibos had to learn to be traders or go hungry. By now they have ranged all over the country. There are Ibo clan unions in all the major cities.

While you search for work you and other young school-leavers will do everything you can to further your education. You will take correspondence courses. You will take typing lessons. If you are especially gifted, you might win a government scholarship for high school and beyond. In the meantime, you keep looking for a job. But it sometimes becomes very discouraging.

Many idealistic young people today become embittered when

the world frustrates them so. Surprisingly enough, Nigeria's young school-leavers are, for the most part, optimistic. They have great faith in their country. They trust their leaders. Even though things may be hard now, they are convinced the future will be better.

Optimism is in the air in Nigeria. Young people are always eager to try their fortune, in spite of the problems they meet. If they stayed on the farm, they would not need to worry much about unemployment, job hunting, and the high cost of living. Farm life is certainly not luxurious, but it is steady and sure.

It is also a little dull. And thousands of young Nigerians prefer to trade a safe, dull country existence for the more glamorous, although insecure, city life. They might know it will be hard to make a go of it—but they are eager and hopeful to try.

This optimistic spirit is one reason why communism has never been a threat in Nigeria. Many Nigerians are poor, to be sure. But what they want is money and influence for themselves. They are not particularly interested in taking it away from the people who have it. They just want a share. And they feel they stand a chance of getting it without resorting to violence and anarchy.

Nigerians everywhere are passionately interested in their nation's progress. With government assistance a company has installed thousands of very low-priced radios throughout the country. Now even in remote villages you might discover a radio speaker in the marketplace. Nigerians who cannot read or write follow the news closely. Most important, they feel their leaders are working for them. Whatever their problems may be, they feel their country is doing the best it can for them.

Nigeria is really a democratic country—not just because its government is so, but because any young person with energy and education can rise to the top. In fact, most of Nigeria's leaders today come from very simple backgrounds. It is their education and drive which gave them influence and prestige, not their family connections. That is why young men and women there feel hopeful in spite of all the difficulties they face. They see so many others who became successful with nothing more to start with than they have.

It is energetic optimism like this which builds a strong young country.

13
agriculture

NIGERIA IS an agricultural country, and most Nigerians are farmers. The country's economy is founded on agriculture. The three most important crops are palm kernels, peanuts, and cocoa, accounting for over three-fourths of Nigeria's exports. You will find, therefore, that their production forms a vital part of the lives of millions of Nigerians.

These three crops correspond roughly to the three regions. Palm kernels come from the thick, lush tropical forest which blankets the Eastern Region. Cocoa is grown primarily in the Western Region. Peanuts come from the drier north. In Nigeria peanuts are called groundnuts, as they are in England.

Nigeria produces great amounts of these crops. It exports more palm oil and palm kernels, for example, than any other country in the world. It is also the world's largest exporter of peanuts. It is the world's third largest producer of cocoa.

The oil palm might almost be said to be Nigeria's national plant. Like the proverbial pig, no part of it is wasted. The stalk fibers are used for building houses. The fronds are used to thatch roofs. The juice of the stalk makes a favorite beverage called palm wine. When crushed, the fleshy casement of the kernels yields a very valuable oil. Another oil comes from the kernels themselves.

113

These oils are very important in making soap, margarine, and candles, and Nigeria exports enough of them to supply every person in England with a cake of soap and a quarter pound of margarine a week!

It was this palm produce which originally drew the European traders deeper and deeper into the interior. It was because the trade was so rich that the different countries competed so fiercely among themselves to dominate the market.

Cocoa was introduced into Nigeria in the nineteenth century and developed purely for export. Nigeria now grows one-seventh of all the cocoa in the world. Cocoa, or cacao, trees look some-

Dismantling a pyramid of peanuts for export overseas.

thing like white birches with large orange-colored pods, the cocoa seed, growing on their branches. It is the Western Region's most important crop.

Peanuts are the Northern Region's big export crop. One of the most typical sights in Nigeria is the huge pyramids around Kano, each one built of 10,400 large sacks of shelled peanuts. From a distance they look almost like the Egyptian pyramids of Giza. This is how the crop is stored until it is shipped to the seaports in the south for export overseas.

In addition to these vital export crops, Nigeria grows most of its own food. Countries like England or Cuba, for example, would starve if they were cut off from the outside world, because they must import so much of their food. Nigeria, however, could still eat because most of its food is grown at home.

Nigerians in the north grow and eat a lot of grain, particularly wheat and millet. Rice is well suited to the Eastern Region because that area is so moist. People in the southern areas grow many tropical fruits and vegetables, too. Bananas, papaws, and cassava root are popular. Cassava root has to be dried first, then grated, and finally fried. Usually a kerosene tin which has been roughed up with hammer and nails is used to grate it.

The most famous food of the south, however, is the yam. Yams grow underground and they look like enormous shaggy sweet potatoes. They are the staple food of millions of West Africans. Foo-foo is the traditional dish, made of yams pounded to a pulp and then cooked with spices. When it is finished, foo-foo makes a whitish and rather rubbery mound. Traditionally you are expected to eat it with your fingers. But a lot of people now use a knife and fork. You are supposed to tear off a hunk from the central dish, dip it into the stew bowl, and swallow it without chewing.

Kola nuts are a national delicacy. They grow mostly in the

Eastern Region, and they are shipped all over the country. They are a little larger than a tennis ball, with a reddish rough surface. Inside there are several sections. These nuts are offered to a guest when he enters your home, and they are eaten as a part of the ceremony at important gatherings in the Eastern Region. You will find them for sale in every marketplace. Chewing a kola nut satisfies both hunger and thirst; and it acts as a stimulant too, the way coffee does, because the nuts are very high in caffeine. Don't chew too many, though, because they will turn your teeth black!

Meat is very rare except in the north. There you will find herds of cattle and goats and other animals. But in the south the fever-bearing tsetse fly kills almost all livestock. People in the south, therefore, eat very little meat. But they do have a lot of dried fish.

Since independence the Nigerian Government has launched a big campaign to improve the people's diet which, throughout the country, and particularly in the south, is quite unbalanced. Many Ibo babies in the Eastern Region, for instance, are raised almost completely on foo-foo. The daily diet is deficient in so many vital nutrients that thousands of people suffer from diseases caused by malnutrition. Until recently thousands of children died before they were five years old.

Hundreds of mobile clinics have now been sent out into the "bush." (The back country all over Africa is called bush.) These little clinics are usually manned by only one busy doctor with perhaps a volunteer assistant, a box of medications, and a baby scale.

The clinic truck arrives on a certain day of the week. The mothers bring their children in from miles away to be examined. The clinics weigh the babies, examine them, and give their

Free clinical care is available to all expectant mothers.

mothers instructions on how to feed and care for them until the next clinic day.

Progress is slow. It is very hard to change people's eating habits because their traditions are centuries old. It takes a lot of time and effort to convince them that many of their diseases could be prevented with a change of diet. But slowly the educational clinics are succeeding. The babies they care for become visibly healthier. Other mothers see this and bring their babies in. Gradually the word spreads and the grip of hunger and disease on a community is eventually broken.

People in Nigeria almost always buy their food in enormous open-air marketplaces instead of in stores as we do. Markets are held on particular days of the week all over Nigeria. Farmers and traders sometimes come from miles away to attend them. Some of the markets are no more than tiny gatherings under the village council tree; others sprawl over many acres of open space. The most famous of these are the great markets in Kano in the Northern Region, Ibadan in the Western Region, and in Onitsha in the Eastern Region. The tremendous Onitsha market has been roofed over by the city to protect it from the weather.

A market is a very exciting place. Everything imaginable is displayed for sale, from camels to soap, from bananas to needles, airplane parts and witchcraft supplies, yams, detergents, sewing machines and Coca-Cola—the variety is endless. Tom-tom drummers and musicians wander through the crowds playing for the money people throw them. The air is thick with hundreds of different smells and sounds.

Ibadan's open market is one of the largest in Africa.

The big markets are divided into several sections, according to the items for sale. You buy food in one place, livestock in another, tools somewhere else, and so on. In the great Onitsha market the merchants lease their booths for a definite length of time, and the market police are kept busy chasing away unauthorized traders who set up without a lease wherever business is good. In the other markets you can set up anywhere you please.

It really takes very little to go into business in a market. First you find a large firm which will sell you a basic stock of their items on credit. Then you just go to the market and sell it. As in every business, the more energetic you are, and the better you can judge what the public wants, the more money you will make.

You will notice one thing which may surprise you—a great many of the tradespeople are women. These market women, especially in the big southern cities, are a lively, strong-minded, and uninhibited group of ladies. Many of them might be illiterate, but they are shrewd businesswomen. Some of them have made tidy fortunes starting with little capital but much enterprise.

They are a vocal and influential lot, these market women. If they do not like something the government is doing, they make it known in no uncertain terms. An unpopular tax can prompt them to stage sit-down demonstrations which will stop traffic for hours. They will organize rallies for joint action. If they do not like a speaker, they will heckle him unmercifully. And since many of them have a huge sense of humor and no qualms about speaking their minds, they can be a stiff challenge to any speaker's self-possession.

These market women have represented an important part of Nigeria's commercial system since the earliest days of trading in the south. One of them, Mme. Tinubu, became a millionairess

With few exceptions, stall-keepers in the open markets are women.

in the 1860's and even became a silent power behind the government in her native city. She was also influential in Lagos politics of the time. Tinubu Square in Lagos is named after her.

With respect to women, the markets of the north are quite a contrast. You see almost no market women there. The ones you do see are either very young—less than fourteen or so—or a good deal older—say, over forty-five.

Why? Because orthodox Moslem wives are in purdah—religiously "secluded." It is not considered proper for a married Moslem woman to be seen in public. Moreover she marries young—fourteen is the usual age—and so you will see few women in the marketplaces. The young ones are not yet married, and the older ones are either widowed or divorced.

Now, if you want to buy something in any marketplace, north or south, there is one thing to remember. Never pay the first price asked. No one expects you to, and you will be immediately tagged as a greenhorn and a fool if you do. You must haggle and bargain spiritedly for some time before you and the merchant settle on a price.

Don't be surprised if it is much lower than the original price he quoted. He would be startled if you paid his first price without question, and he purposely makes it high so he has plenty of room for bargaining.

14

marketing boards

THE MARKETS handle only retail trade. They have nothing to do with the large-scale wholesale marketing of Nigeria's basic export crops. This enormous task is completely in the hands of the government-controlled Regional Marketing Boards. Only the Marketing Boards may buy and export cocoa, palm oil and kernels, peanuts, cotton, soybeans, and citrus fruit. That does not cover everything Nigeria exports, but it does include every item of major importance.

What are the Marketing Boards? They serve as a guaranteed customer for every farmer who grows the items under their jurisdiction. If the farmer's crop meets the proper standards, the Regional Marketing Board will buy it all from him. He need not worry that his harvest will rot in the field for want of a buyer.

The boards also use their reserve funds to cushion drastic variations in world prices. The farmer does not need to worry that a sudden price drop will bankrupt him. If the world price slumps sharply, the boards will lower the price gradually for a year or two and give the farmer a chance to switch to growing something else.

It was not always like this. Before World War II the farmer's life was a precarious one. The prices of agricultural commodities often fluctuate widely from year to year. One year a farmer might sell his crop for a good profit, but the next year he might not be able to find any buyer for it at all. If and when that happened, he and his family had to go hungry. Most Nigerian farms are very small, usually only a few acres worked by the whole family, including the children. Such a small farmer is unable to build up a financial backlog for emergencies. The farmer lived from year to year. One bad year could mean great hardship—even disaster.

Shipping costs also eat into the farmer's profit. Nigeria is a very big country, as big as France and Italy combined. But the country's only ports are in the south. Anything produced for export, therefore, must be transported to the coast. If it must travel a long distance, just the cost of getting it to the place where it can reach an overseas buyer can be very expensive. If the price is low to begin with, this does not leave much for the farmer himself.

A giant corporation or large-scale producer could bargain for the price it demands. It could hold out for a higher price, or it could try to undersell its competitors by using its reserve funds from previous years. But the average Nigerian farmer has no such economic power. He is small and he is still comparatively isolated, in spite of the improvements in communications during the past few years.

The Marketing Boards do the job of a farmers' trade union. They can bargain with authority because they represent most of the farmers in the region. By being so big, the boards can exert the economic influence that the individual farmer could never have.

Everyone raising cocoa for export, for instance, sells his crop to his Regional Marketing Board and to no one else. That means anyone wanting to buy cocoa must come to the Cocoa Board for it. That board commands the cocoa crop of an entire region. It has, therefore, a great deal of bargaining power. It illustrates the old saying that in unity there is strength.

The Marketing Boards began during World War II. Until then, Nigeria's export trade was controlled completely by foreign-owned private firms. They bought the crops from the individual producer and arranged for their shipment and sale overseas. Any profits, naturally, went to the shareholders in the company. Since these were rarely native Nigerians, it meant that very little of the profits from Nigeria's own produce was used to improve Nigeria itself.

It was bad enough for the economy that agricultural prices could vary so widely. World War II, however, disrupted world trade so severely that for a time it looked as if Nigeria's exports might not find any buyers at all.

This was clearly a national emergency. To cope with it, the British Government stepped in. It guaranteed to buy the country's entire cocoa crop at fixed prices. The Cocoa Control Board was then set up in 1940 to market the crop.

Japan entered World War II in 1941, and in one way, at least, this resulted in a benefit for Nigeria. Japan's initial military successes cut off the Allies' access to the vegetable oils from the Far East. Thus, the oils from Nigeria's peanuts and palm produce suddenly became vital to the war effort. They were added to the national control arrangements already set up for cocoa.

This automatically removed the fear that a crop would not sell. Instead, bigger crops were needed. For the first time, an individual producer could count on a stable price for his goods. He could be sure of selling his crop when it was ripe. And this served as an incentive to invest his time and financial reserves in increasing his future production.

These wartime produce-control arrangements proved so successful that they were continued after the war ended. More and more crops were added to the list. For more efficient operation, Regional Marketing Boards were set up in their present form in 1954.

How do the Marketing Boards work? At the beginning of each buying season a fixed price is announced for each item. Hundreds of government buying stations are set up throughout the country where farmers may bring their produce for grading and sale. If he wishes, a farmer may sell his crop to a middleman who will then bring it to the buying station and take a commission from the proceeds for himself.

When the produce is brought to the buying station, it is graded and sealed by inspection teams from the Produce Inspection Services. These teams are responsible for enforcing the official grades and quality standards set up by the Marketing Boards.

The Government guarantees to buy everything which meets its standards. Higher prices are paid for better produce. Originally only a small percentage of the total crop qualified as first-grade. Now the majority of each crop does. The premium grade for cocoa was abolished a few years after it was started, because the crop improved so much that it was all graded as premium quality.

When quality improves this way, it means that Nigerian products bring better prices on the competitive world market. That means the farmers themselves make more money. It also brings more business to Nigeria as a whole, because it builds a reputation for fine produce which the government is careful to maintain.

The Marketing Boards operate through government-licensed buying agents. These are all reliable, experienced commercial firms, with solid backgrounds in the produce trade. These licensed agents are responsible for everything concerning the crops they handle: producer payments, labeling, packing, transport, and delivery. They are completely answerable for their goods until they deliver them at the port of shipment. Then they are paid in the form of a "buying allowance." The allowance covers normal expenses and provides them a fair profit in return for their services.

The boards keep a surplus fund on hand to cushion the producer from too sudden price variations. If the price drops sharply one year, the boards will make up some of the difference out of their own funds so the small farmer will have a chance to plant something more profitable the next year. On the other hand, if prices rise, the boards use part of the increase in revenue to replenish their reserve funds, part of it to raise the price paid to the farmer, and the rest to finance research.

The latter item is a very important advantage of this system. Research is vital to improve farming methods and plant varieties. But research is very expensive. It would be very difficult to find the money for it any other way. The Marketing Boards, however, are able to finance this vital work from the sale of Nigerian commodities overseas. The boards are now required by law to set aside 22½ per cent of their net profits for research and development projects.

The Marketing Boards system gives unity to Nigerian agriculture. The only other way this could have been done would be to replace the traditional small farms with large plantations. Giant plantations are of course more efficient than tiny farms, just as an assembly-line factory is more efficient than a small workshop. But replacing the traditonal individual farm with such large-scale plantations would seriously disrupt the farmer's ancient way of life.

The repercussions from such a change might upset a nation's whole way of life. While admittedly it might succeed in increasing production, it would surely create untold unhappiness and social discontent. Russia tried it in the 1930's. The peasants burned their land and killed their livestock in their effort to resist collectivization. China has tried it more recently. But their experiment is working badly too. People just will not work for the state the way they would for themselves.

The Marketing Boards, therefore, have managed to improve quality and raise production without robbing the individual farmer of incentive and his feeling of independence.

Gradually the ancient system of tiny fragmented holdings will give way to a more modern arrangement. Even with the way production has increased since 1940, bigger crops will be needed as Nigeria's population and export trade expand. Tiny individual farms cannot produce efficiently and they cannot afford the machinery which modern farming requires. But it is far better that the change be gradual, as it is now. Sudden drastic changes create more problems than they can solve.

Nigeria's young people will have a strong influence in changing Nigerian agriculture. In the schools today, they are beginning to learn modern agricultural techniques. They are discovering the greater opportunities of today's world and they want their share of them. It may be true that the rigidity of a traditional farming system will not permit them to practice fully their new farming know-how for the time being. Sooner or later, however, this new generation will start to remodel Nigerian farming. Not because they will be forced to do it, but because they will want to do it.

15

the
northern
region

YOU ALREADY KNOW a lot about the Northern Region. You have learned something of its history, which is quite independent of the rest of the country. You know a little of its religion. You have met its women and seen how its people dress. Let us visit certain places there and fill out your picture. The logical place to begin is the wonderful old city of Kano.

Kano is the most famous city in Northern Nigeria. It is located just about exactly in the center of the Northern Region.

Wood is scarce in the dry, sun-baked north, so Kano is built entirely of mud. But what they can do with mud! The city walls are solid mud—forty feet thick and pierced with several gates that lead into the city itself. Kano was an impregnable fortress in earlier times. Inside the huge walls are large open spaces with ponds where the goats drink. If Kano was besieged, it could even grow food inside its defenses on these open stretches of land.

The city proper has one of the most fascinating architectural styles in the world. Nearly all the houses are flat-roofed mud structures with little pointed spires sticking up at the corners. Before the mud dries, all kinds of patterns in a variety of colors are drawn into it. The design is purely up to the owner's imagination. You will see complicated geometrical figures, strange birds, exotic flowers, curious cross-hatching, and serpentine curlicues. Sometimes the twentieth century makes itself felt and a small airplane or a steamship will appear along with the other designs. To complete the effect, the house itself may be painted in different colors for a thoroughly individual result.

Every Moslem city has at least one mosque. But the mosque at Kano is the best known in Nigeria. It is an impressive white building with a blue-green dome. Four tall white towers, called

The clustered mud-walled houses in Kano's Old City.

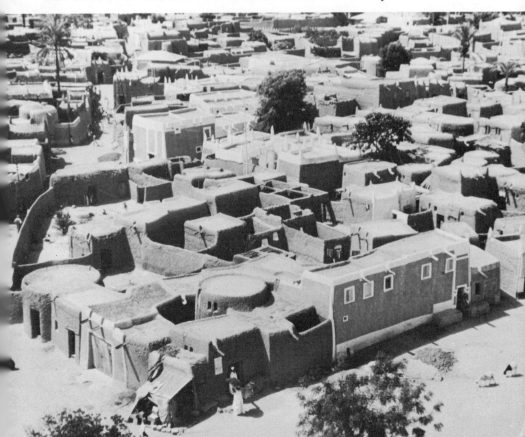

The colors and designs of Kano's mud-walled homes reflect individualism and artistic expression.

minarets, stand at its corners. Religion here is so important in everyday life that this handsome mosque was built with British Government funds, almost like a public works project.

The Koran instructs all pious Moslems to pray five times daily while facing Mecca, the holy city of Islam where Mohammed lived and taught. So five times a day, the muezzin, or Moslem priest, mounts to the top of one of the minarets and calls the Faithful to prayer. His song is high and clear and beautiful in the bright, hot air. It is amplified with powerful loudspeakers.

Friday is the Moslem sabbath. And the Friday noon prayer session is a special affair. From every direction people converge on the big square in front of the mosque. A Moslem must never pray on the bare ground, so each one brings a prayer rug on which he kneels. Some are little more than rags. Others are rich and beautifully woven with geometrical designs, animals and flowers. You will not see pictures of men, however. The Koran forbids Moslems to depict the human figure because it considers that to be idolatrous.

Gradually the enormous square fills up. Some of the worshipers arrive on bicycles, which they park right in the middle of the crowd wherever they find space. It is a fascinating scene—hundreds of men in white robes kneeling and touching their foreheads to the ground. The hot bright desertlike sun beats down, casting sharp black shadows, and the red goats forage around the edges of the square.

Thousands gather before Kano's Great Mosque for the Friday noon prayer session.

There are goats everywhere. In small workshops near the marketplace you can see why. There you will see crews of men curing goatskins. They bleach them and scrape off the reddish-brown hair. The hides are chemically treated until they are pure white.

Kano is a very ancient trading center, and for many centuries it was the southern end of a great trade route stretching northward across the Sahara all the way to the Mediterranean. Arab caravans traveled regularly across the desert, often loaded exclusively with the fine goatskins of Kano, which were sold to merchants in the markets of Morocco. It was here that Europeans in the Middle Ages bought goatskins, and that is how they came to be called Moroccan leather.

Another ancient Kano product has also been famous for centuries in West Africa. That is its deep blue cloth. Just inside Kano's city walls there are dozens of vat holes in the ground which are filled with an inky indigo dye. Nearly any time of day you will see men squatting next to the pits, dipping lengths of cloth into the dye until the fabric reaches just the right shade of blue. Then they beat the cloth with mallets coated with butter and glue. This gives it a shiny, polished look. The finished cloth is highly prized even in this day of mass-produced textiles.

Nigerians in the south are very lively, outgoing people. They are extremely friendly and fun-loving. In the north, dignity and decorum are more esteemed than animation and activity. The Moslems in the north, especially the Fulani, are more reserved than their countrymen to the south. A man is expected to know his own worth and to respect his superiors.

The Fulani men's flowing robes and neat skullcaps enhance their dignified appearance. It is a very flattering costume. It shows off a man's good bearing the way the Roman toga did.

Fulani men tend to keep somewhat to themselves. In the

Tribesmen ride camels in the desert expanses on the Northern Region.

marketplaces all over Nigeria, for instance, you will usually see them standing together a little away from the core of the crowd. They are excellent businessmen, however. So don't be fooled by their cool exterior.

Learning is highly respected among Nigeria's Moslems. A scholar is respectfully called *mallam,* which means "teacher." Many boys attend the traditional Koranic schools, although as yet very few girls are given such education.

These schools concentrate primarily upon Koranic teachings. Only recently have the Moslems begun to consider any other kind of learning worth while. Religion is the center of their lives and so they regard it as the most necessary sort of education.

Arabic is taught in Moslem schools in the Northern Region.

There are thousands of small Koranic schools all over northern Nigeria. Every year after the harvest, the mallam leaves his farm and tours his neighborhood, collecting pupils for the coming year. The boys come to live with him and help on his farm. Their parents pay the mallam a fee. In return, he instructs their sons in the wisdom of Islam.

The schools are very simple. The boys sit crosslegged on the ground in the open. Each one has a small slate on which he copies out passages from the Koran while the mallam supervises.

At first the boys learn the Koran by heart. The Koran is written in Arabic. Arabic is not a Nigerian language, so the boys do not understand the meaning of what they memorize. But nevertheless they commit it to memory, learn it word for word. When they have mastered this, they are entitled to call themselves mallam and take pupils of their own. It does not matter if they do not understand the Arabic words they teach. The holy words of the Koran are considered so powerful that it is enough to be able to repeat them correctly. The boys who go further in their studies learn the Arabic language itself. They also begin to study the meaning and background of the Koran.

The mallams are widely believed to have magical powers in making charms. These charms consist of passages from the Koran written on paper and tied up in a little packet of cloth. They are highly esteemed as protection against evil forces.

It is no wonder the mallams are so respected. After all, they know the mighty words of the holy Koran. And most of them know how to write, an attainment that has always been regarded with great awe. The Koran is regarded as the law of life. Even the water used to erase a Koranic passage from a slate is thought to have magical powers. Many people drink it every morning.

This attitude toward writing even affected nineteenth-century European politics. Toward the end of the century Britain and France were arguing over which one would control the northwest part of Nigeria. Both countries sent expeditions hot-foot through the region. They were to get signed trade treaties from all the local chieftains as fast as they could. When the British appeared, seemingly from nowhere, and requested the ruler to sign his name on a mysterious piece of paper, the people were positive this was intended as sorcery against their king. The king's name was almost sacred to begin with, but to write it down was clearly magic!

So the British never saw the real king. One of his ministers would pretend to be the ruler. He would sign the treaty, all right. But he would use an imaginary name.* When this fact

* The French were less polite. They used guns and threats, and they got the king's real name. But as soon as they took away their guns, he threw away their treaty!

became known, it thoroughly confused all the negotiations between Britain and France over their rival claims. A very ancient belief had some very modern consequences.

The southern portion of the tremendous Northern Region is often called the Middle Belt. It is a large stretch of land extending across the middle of Nigeria. About the time Nigeria gained its independence from Britain, many people wanted to create a separate Middle Belt State because this area is so very different from the rest of Northern Nigeria.

Although the Fulani conquered this land in the early nineteenth century, it is still largely pagan, not Moslem. Its people belong to many different unrelated tribes, even though the ruling class is Fulani. Many of them live isolated in the hills. Up to now they have remained nearly untouched by modern influences. They are shy people, still living a wild, free, and often primitive life.

The conquering Fulani were a proud people. They looked down on their pagan subjects. Being Moslem themselves, they firmly believed that pagans were less than human. They raided them mercilessly for slaves. They devastated whole regions, destroying towns and selling thousands of people into slavery. Even now in the Middle Belt you can see the ruins of once-thriving towns which were obliterated in the slave raids of the nineteenth century.

These slave raids were a great curse throughout West Africa. Northern Nigeria was particularly hard hit. The British had managed to bring slaving along the coast under control by mid-nineteenth century. But not until the opening of the twentieth century was it possible to stop it in the north.

The Fulani enslaved many Moslems too. Even those not captured were often ruined by the enormous cost of ransoming their relatives, that is, if they could be found and the ransom accepted.

One of the states in the Middle Belt was called Kontagora. The emir of this state was so feared for his slave raids that he was nicknamed "The Destroyer." Curiously, he was very proud of the title. The British tried to make him stop his slaving. But he just jeered at them. "Can you stop a cat from mousing?" he said. "When I die, it will be with a slave in my mouth!"

About the turn of the century the British were able to crack down on the northern slave trade. But it was harder to eliminate slavery itself. It could not be done all at once. Trade, business, and home life all depended upon it. If all slaves had suddenly been freed, the whole economy would have collapsed.

The first step was a law which made it impossible to force a runaway slave to return to his master. If he managed to escape, he was legally free. Finally, a law decreed that all children of slave parents who were born after a specific date were deemed free.

Right in the center of the Middle Belt is the great Jos plateau. Nigeria's important tin deposits are here. Nigeria is one of the world's largest producers of tin. You might think of a tin mine as a deep tunnel in the earth, like a coal mine. In the Jos tin mines, however, the metal is contained in a heavy black sand which is at the surface of the ground. You dig just a little way and there you have it.

This central plateau region is far less arid than the land farther north. The scenery is beautiful. There are gently rolling hills dotted with trees, which you rarely see up north. One has the feeling of green and gold open spaces stretching to a far horizon. This quiet, peaceful belt of land is an unexpected surprise to those who have seen only the lush tropical growth of the coast or the sunbaked north.

No tour of Northern Nigeria is complete without a *durbar*. A durbar is a great festival. It is held in honor of some important event in the Northern Region. For example, there are durbars for the birthday of the Sardauno of Sokoto, to honor a visiting dignitary, or to observe the anniversary of national independence. The highlight of the proceedings is the grand charge of Fulani horsemen.

Fulani cavalrymen are impressive figures. They look very romantic in their sweeping dark robes. They have an air of mystery, too, because their heavy turbans have a tail of fabric which veils the lower part of their faces.

Horses are gaily caparisoned on festive occasions in the Northern Region.

A true Fulani is a superb horseman, and the durbar is a rousing spectacle. The horsemen thunder across the field at full gallop, straight at the guests of honor. Just when it seems they will trample the guests to death, the riders rein to a sudden stop only yards from the reviewing stand! The whole thundering charge stops on a dime, as it were, and the horsemen shout their salute.

The Fulani horsemen do not have it all to themselves at a durbar. Everybody has a hand in the festivities. There is dancing, music, and drumming. The markets do a roaring business. There is every imaginable kind of entertainment, and the whole festival can go on for days. But the big event is the proud trumpet fanfare and that pounding cavalry charge.

At some of the very special durbars the Fulani riders will wear chain mail with their heavy robes. This armor is startlingly like medieval European mail you may see in our museums. It is, indeed, derived from the European model.

Some seven hundred years ago, the Crusaders came to North Africa with their flexible and beautiful chain mail. They had little effect on Moslem power in North Africa, but their wonderful armor was copied by their enemies. In later years the Moslems themselves swept southward into Africa. They brought with them the chain mail and horse armor they had adopted many years before from the Crusaders.

So you can see it now at a durbar in northern Nigeria— medieval armored knights saluting a twentieth-century celebrity, while the crowd throngs about you, with uniformed soldiers and Fulani nomads, Arab merchants and southerners in Western-style suits, and perhaps an airplane or two overhead. Everywhere you look the present and the past are blended in a fascinating, endlessly surprising mixture.

That is Nigeria's Northern Region.

16

the
eastern
region

FROM THE HOT, sprawling brightness of the north, let us travel on to the green forested Eastern Region. You are no stranger to the east by now, either. You have visited its famous market-place of Onitsha on the Niger River. You have seen some of the problems facing a young man of the Ibo tribe there. You have seen how its rich palm produce attracted European traders for centuries and finally brought it under British rule. So let us take yet another journey through this part of Nigeria and see some places we have missed.

This is Iboland, for the Ibos are the largest group in the Eastern Region. A celebration is going on. It is the "official" funeral of an important chief. He may have died quite a while ago. Perhaps his body has actually been buried a long time. Until his family has enough money for a big funeral, however, he is not considered properly laid to rest.

A proper funeral, moreover, is expensive. For one thing, it must necessarily include an enormous feast for the entire vil-lage, with lots of beer and foamy palm wine.

Palm wine, a great favorite in Nigeria, is made from the juice of the oil palm stalk. You can buy it at little booths in nearly any market place. It is one of the indispensable bridal gifts any hopeful young suitor must give to his bride's family. No celebration would be complete without it.

Beer is just as popular. Nearly every place in Africa has its own local brewery. You can sample as many beers in Africa as in Germany! Africans also like Coca-Cola, Pepsi-Cola and 7-Up as much as we do. So a proper funeral must include substantial supplies of soft drinks, too.

In the old days a chief had to be accompanied to the underworld by an impressive retinue of wives and slaves. That was to ensure his being recognized as a personage of importance. It was believed that only then would he be reborn in favorable circumstances.

Slave dealing flourished because of this belief. True, the Fulani raiders never penetrated the tropical forest. So the Fulani slavers never preyed upon the people of the Eastern Region. There were hundreds of other slavers along the coast, however. And since victims were always needed for sacrifice at an important person's funeral, slave raiding became a dreadful scourge.

It was terrible to kill so many people to provide ghostly attendants for a dead chief. The motive was not brutality, however. People believed deeply that their chief must be properly recognized in the land of the dead. If he was not, he might be reborn as a beggar or even as a slave. That would bring shame and disgrace to his tribe as well as to his family. So to prove how important he had been in life, his people made sure he was accompanied by as many attendants as possible in his journey to the underworld.

The sacrificing of slaves has, of course, long since been outlawed. But a lavish funeral is still a must for anyone of importance. No expense is spared. There is food and drink, singing and dancing and drumming. And for a deceased man of special

Ancient masks reflect influence of animals in native arts.

prominence, his clan's dreaded ancestral spirits may make an appearance to honor his funeral.

And here they come! Their costumes are fantastic. They wear towering carved masks. Some advance with dignity; others make terrifying and threatening gestures. When they speak, their voices are high, rasping, and unearthly.

The costumes are incredibly varied. Some encase the masquerader's body entirely in rope mesh with great grass ruffs at the neck and ankles. Others are hoop skirts, six feet in width— or splendid painted cloth robes ornamented with bells and beads. Often the costume will encase the wearer's head to make him look taller. Then he must look out through eye holes cut in the chest.

The variety is endless. But all these costumes are believed to have magical powers woven into them. They are sacred articles, not just fancy dress. Only the men who have been initiated into the clan's religious secrets may wear them.

The masks are works of art. Often they are as much as three feet tall. The carving is very intricate. The faces show innumerable variations in expression. Some have great pointed fangs to give the impression of strength. Others have huge staring eyes or enormous beaklike noses.

Some of the faces are stark white. This has been the symbol of the powerful dead for many centuries. When these people first saw white men, they were frightened by the color of their skins. They thought they were dead spirits come to life.

The masquerader's voice is disguised too. He talks through a narrow tube with a piece of cobweb tied across one end. This gives his voice a grating, inhuman quality. For a long time this was one of the most closely guarded religious secrets of all. It was this terrible voice which completed the guise of the supernatural.

In earlier times only those who had been initiated into the tribe's religious cult were permitted to see these "spirits." Anyone else who saw them was put to death for sacrilege. To warn the people they were coming, the masqueraders used a noisemaker called a bull-roarer. It was a long narrow piece of wood which was twirled at the end of a string. It made a loud roaring noise which told everyone to run for his life and hide his face. It was especially taboo for women to see the spirits. Women were never initiated into the religious cults.

But the old religion has been greatly weakened now. The spirits do not seem so awesome any more. Once it was believed that when a masquerader put on his sacred costume, he actually assumed the character of the spirit he represented. Now he is still a man. The old magic is gone.

People still treat masqueraders with respect, of course. They make a show of running away to a discreet distance when they hear the bull-roarer. But gradually the masqueraders are becoming just men dressed up in wonderful costumes, not mighty spirits whose appearance is both a great honor and a great terror.

The Eastern Region comprises the heart of the palm belt. The forest is like hot green lace. The palm trees filter the fierce tropical sun into a thick green twilight. The tall trees surround you on every side. They meet above your head in intricate interweaving designs. Shiny brown kernels grow in spiky clusters on the trees. These little kernels have written a great deal of Nigeria's history.

Some of the palm oil is still obtained by the old primitive hand-crushing methods. But more and more large modern processing plants are being built throughout the country. These new plants are much more efficient than the old methods: they extract more of the oil from the kernels, and of course they can handle great quantities at a time. It is another of Nigeria's contrasts that the palm kernels are grown in the eternal, unchanging forest and end up in these huge modern processing plants.

Palm oil is not the only oil the Eastern Region possesses. If you travel south to the coast you will find the busy, growing city of Port Harcourt. Here important petroleum deposits have been discovered, and a great new refinery has been built.

Port Harcourt is a very young city. The British began its construction after coal was discovered near Enugu, in the center of the Eastern Region. A railroad was built to serve the new coal fields. Port Harcourt was the southern end of this railroad. It is now the second largest port in Nigeria. (Lagos is of course the biggest.)

There is nothing quaint about Port Harcourt. Everything is businesslike. It is not a particularly pretty town. But then, it was never meant to be a tourist attraction. It is a world-wide trade center. The important thing is to get the huge ships unloaded and reloaded. No one has time for sightseeing.

The Eastern Region has had a big job to do in developing its resources. It has very poor soil. The thick forest has always hindered communications. Until lately, except in the cities, its people have been isolated from the modern world.

Its people, however, are enthusiastically willing to help themselves. Its villages and families are very closely knit. Each person feels strongly responsible for helping his whole group, so they get together and do things to help one another.

Scores of little villages have started their own self-improvement programs. Every member of the community must contribute a share of the money needed. Also he must help out whenever labor is required. A whole village will get together to clear the site for a new school. Everyone will turn out to build a bridge. The local bicycle track will be widened and a new road built.

More and more of the young people of the Eastern Region are entering government and the professional fields. New investment is attracted by the region's rapid growth. A big new cement factory has been built at Nkalagu. Aluminum investment and oil companies are all interested in this active area.

Ambition for the future and eagerness to help itself characterize Eastern Nigeria.

17

the western region and lagos

HANG ON to your hat! This mammy wagon is going places! It has no shock absorbers to speak of, so keep a firm grip on your goat, too—and your chickens, lunch, babies, knapsack and everything else this wagon is bursting with. Mammy-wagon drivers are enthusiastic to say the least. They are not interested in cushioning the bumps for you.

What is a mammy wagon? It's a public bus. Usually, the bus is only a truck with benches in the back, a tarpaulin stretched over the top, a bright coat of paint, and a large slogan painted prominently to complete the effect. The slogan is anything that appeals to the driver, from a Biblical quotation to a private joke. Examples: "God Is Love," "No Sweet, No Sweat," "The Lord Is Our Shepherd," "In God We Trust, But Don't Trust Women."

This is the way most Nigerians travel, particularly in the south where roads are more plentiful. Riding in a mammy wagon is likely to be bumpy, but it will very likely be cheery too. Nigerians are very friendly company.

By our standards Nigerians are startlingly hospitable. For one thing, they are very good-natured people. But they have a tradition of hospitality too. Family relationships are highly valued, even very distant ones. Nigerians do not mind having unexpected company. Relatives are always turning up from no-where, but they are always welcome. And scores of relations turn out to send a traveler on his journey—even a short trip.

You are entering Yoruba country now. If you should strike up a conversation with a total stranger, and if you take a liking to each other, he is quite likely to invite you home to dinner and entertain you royally. This might surprise you. But your Nigerian friend is much more easygoing about it. If he likes you, he acts accordingly.

You can feel a whole different atmosphere in the south. By comparison, the north seems sedate and conservative. The southerner's tempo of life is quicker. People are more animated. They joke and laugh more easily. They also question authority more quickly. For many years the nationalist movement was strongest in the Western Region. It is also the most westernized of the three regions.

Local buses are called "Mammy Wagons."

The capital of the Western Region is Ibadan, the most populous city built by Africans south of the Sahara. Like Kano and Benin, Ibadan existed centuries before the white man came. Many Westerners think Africans never created cities of their own. But nothing could be farther from the truth. Ibadan with a population of over half a million is a big, sprawling place—a truly African city, founded and peopled almost exclusively by Africans.

From the air, Ibadan looks like a sea of corrugated tin roofs. These roofs are really its trademark. The older portions of the city form an incredibly complicated maze of family compounds. Like most West Africans, Yorubas like to live in big family groups around a common courtyard. Ibadan has hundreds of such compounds.

In contrast to these sections of the city stand the shining modern office buildings of the business section. Like every important city in Nigeria, Ibadan is in the midst of a phenomenal building boom. It started with independence in 1960. Hundreds of buildings were needed to house the functions of the new government. Then as the flow of business and investment to Nigeria began to speed up, the demand for more and more office buildings and factories, along with houses for the people they employed, grew as well. These new buildings are climbing skyward in every one of Nigeria's cities, particularly in Lagos and the regional capitals.

Ibadan has another trademark of which all Nigeria is proud. This is the famous University College at Ibadan. Any country could well be proud of this fine university. It has an excellent faculty, including some of Africa's outstanding scholars. Its campus is spacious and beautiful. Its library is enormous. Since its foundation in 1948, it has trained young Nigerians as exact-

Entrance to the University College in Ibadan.

ingly as any of the older colleges of Europe and America. Ibadan is also the site of Africa's first television broadcasting station.

Take a drive now through the Western Region's great cocoa-raising areas. Cocoa is Western Nigeria's basic crop. There are miles and miles of farms raising it.

It is hard to realize as you look at this peaceful land that only 150 years ago it was tortured by the terrors of war and slave raiding. Slave trading flourished in Western Nigeria just as it did everywhere else in West Africa. It thrived because it was so profitable. People do not always realize that Africans themselves were some of the most enthusiastic traders in African slaves. The white man's role was undeniably shameful, but thousands of African slave dealers were equally to blame.

In the early nineteenth century the Yoruba kingdoms were

engaged in an almost never-ending series of long and bloody wars. These were called the Egba Wars. They ruined the once rich Yoruba states. They also caused thousands upon thousands of Nigerians to be sold into slavery. One of these was Samuel Ajayi Crowther, who later became one of the most famous men in Nigerian history.

Crowther was a Yoruba. He was captured when he was very young, sold as a slave and shipped overseas. But on the Atlantic his ship was waylaid by a British vessel. All the slaves were freed.

The rescued slaves were brought back to the free colony of Sierra Leone on the west coast of Africa above Nigeria. England had established Sierra Leone for just this purpose. Missionaries there taught Samuel Crowther how to read and write. They very shortly realized that he was unusually intelligent. They sent him to school in England. There he became an Anglican minister.

Crowther was an important member of the expeditions which explored the Niger in mid-century. He compiled a dictionary of the Yoruba language and became a leading figure in the Christian church in Africa. Finally he reached its pinnacle. He was made a bishop with the title of "Anglican Bishop of Western Equatorial Africa Beyond the Queen's Dominions." Nigerians today think of him as one of their greatest men.

Nigeria has changed beyond all belief in just the century or less since Crowther's day. Nowhere will you see the contrast more clearly than in Lagos.

Lagos is a very modern town. It is busier, faster, and more westernized than most of the rest of Nigeria. It is thoroughly cosmopolitan. Lagosians include members of every major tribe in Nigeria plus Syrians, British, Lebanese, Orientals, Indians— all stirred together in as varied an assortment as you could find anywhere.

Lagos is a collection of contradictions. It has some of Africa's brightest new buildings and some of its worst slums. It is the seat of Nigeria's Federal Government and therefore the symbol of national unity. But it has also seen some of Nigeria's acutest cases of intertribal tensions. Its rich people are some of the country's richest, and its poor people can be poorer than any-where else in the nation. It is one thing to be poor on the land in Nigeria, where your clan or family is there to help you out. At least you know you will not starve. It is something very dif-ferent in the cities where you have cut many of your old ties and you are on your own.

Lagos teems with people, with thousands of bicycles, count-less varieties of costume, scores of different languages. Its harbor is filled with ships from all over the world. Its multilingual radio station broadcasts all sorts of programs in dozens of different dialects. Its newspapers like the Lagos *Times* and the *West African Pilot* are read everywhere in Nigeria and in many other parts of West Africa as well. It even has a brand-new govern-ment-owned television station.

Other cities symbolize Nigeria's past and its tradition. Lagos symbolizes its future—a future with ample educational oppor-tunities for every Nigerian, a future combining the comforts of Western civilization with Africa's time-honored traditions, when every African can point proudly to Nigeria as a strong healthy nation made by his fellow Africans.

This future is in the making right now. Nigeria has just launched an ambitious new nation-wide development plan, mapped out by the Massachusetts Institute of Technology's Center for International Studies. The program covers every aspect of Nigeria's growth for the next six years. Each region and the Federal District of Lagos retains a public relations firm abroad to inform the world of Nigeria's promise and attraction for foreign investment. When we are discouraged by the crises which plague some of the other new African nations, it is heartening to turn to Nigeria as an example to progress. Strong young African nations like this give hope that a stable, democratic Africa will eventually emerge from the troubles of the present. The lessons we can learn from Nigeria can help us cope with the future of the entire continent of Africa.

18

the
mid-western
region

THE MID-WESTERN REGION is the baby of Nigeria. It is the smallest and the youngest of all the regions. Indeed, it is practically newborn, having only been formed in 1963. Formerly it was included in the Western Region.

The Mid-Western Region resembles the Eastern Region in many ways. It is covered with the same thick palm forest and it has the same hot, moist climate. Its people are predominantly Edo, however, and they are very proud indeed of the ancient culture and traditions of their capital city of Benin.

This brand new region faces a huge task in building up its agriculture and industry. To be sure, it has great potential wealth, but it is still the poorest of all the four regions of Nigeria right now. Like all babies, it has to grow up. But it will have help in the form of subsidies from the Federal Government to get on its feet. Big dams, moreover, are now being planned to regularize the flow of the Niger, and when they are completed, the Mid-Western Region will get a good revenue from the traffic back and forth across the great river.

So let's watch it and wish it well. It's a lively youngster, and promises to grow even more so.

19
good-bye

YOU HAVE TRAVELED all over Nigeria. You have met lots of new people. You have looked and listened, tasted and touched. What will you remember most?

Three things will stand out in your memory—Nigeria's diversity, its contrasts, and its promise.

You know now that Nigeria is a mixture of countless traditions, heredities, and backgrounds. You have seen a new country forming before your eyes as this complicated jigsaw merges into a unified nation. Out of all this diversity, a single Nigeria is growing, steadily and confidently.

And the contrasts never cease to surprise you. Old and new, modern and traditional, mingle in an ever fascinating variety. Massive palm oil plants and tiny family-owned hand-operated crushing machines; great ships at Lagos and Port Harcourt, and flimsy canoes ferrying people across the Niger; the beautiful Medical Training College at Lagos, and a makeshift shed in the palm forest where an overworked medical advisor examines babies and pregnant mothers; the huge Kaduna textile mill up north, and the ramshackle looms of village craftsmen; Ibadan's beautifully equipped University College and thousands of open-air schools in the bush whose only textbook is the teacher's blackboard.

Finally there is Nigeria's promise. This is the young giant of Africa's future. It has all the makings of leadership. It is rich in natural resources. It is big and populous. It is politically stable. But most important are its people.

Nigerians are proud of their country. They have faith in their future. They are eager to better themselves. Their energies are poured into improving their lot, not fighting each other.

And it is people who make a nation. After all, faith in your country is only faith in yourself. Optimism and enthusiasm are Nigeria's truest wealth.

Here, then, is a fine and welcome addition to the world's community of nations.

PRONUNCIATIONS

Nnamdi Azikiwe
    NAM-dee a-ZEEK-ee-way
Aba   AH-bah
Benue   BEN-weh
Alhaji Sir Abubakar
  Tafawa Balewa
      al-HAH-gee sir a-BOO-
        bah-kar tah-FAH-wah
        bah-LAY-wah
Benin   BEH-nin
Bonny   BAH-nee
Bida   BEE-dah
calabash   KA-la-bash
cassava   kah-SAH-vah
Samuel Ajayi Crowther
        Samuel ah-JAH-ee
        KROW-ther
Dahomey   dah-HOME-ee
durbar   dur-BAHR
emir   ay-MEER
Enugu   EN-oo-goo
Edo   AY-do
Egba   EGG-bah
Fulani   foo-LAH-nee
harmattan   har-mah-TAHN
Hausa   HOUSE-ah
Ibadan   ee-BAH-dahn
Ibo   EE-bo
Islam   iss-LAHM
Ife   EE-feh

jihad   GEE-hahd
Jos   JAHS
juju   JOO-joo
Kano   KAH-no
Katsina   kat-SEE-nah
Kaduna   kah-DOO-nah
Koran   KO-ran
kola nuts   KO-lah nuts
Kontagora   kon-tah-GO-rah
Lugard   loo-GARD
Lagos   LAY-gos
Mecca   MEK-kah
muezzin   moo-eh-ZEEN
mallam   MAH-lahm
Niger   NI-jer
Nkalagu   nka-LAH-goo
Oyo   OH-yo
Onitsha   oh-NEE-shah
Port Harcourt
        port HAHR-koort
Sardauno   sar-DOO-nah
Sakato   sah-kah-TOO
Sapele   SAH-peh-leh
sabon gari   SAH-bon GAH-ree
Tinubu   tih-NOO-boo
Usman dan Fodio
        OOS-mahn dan
        FO-dee-oh
Yoruba   YOR-oo-bah

INDEX

157